RHAPSODY
IN GREEN

For Max
For Clemmie

RHAPSODY IN GREEN

A novelist, an obsession,
a laughably small excuse for
a vegetable garden

CHARLOTTE MENDELSON

Illustrations by Aitch

KYLE BOOKS

First published in Great Britain in 2016 by
Kyle Books, an imprint of Kyle Cathie Ltd.
192–198 Vauxhall Bridge Road
London SW1V 1DX
general.enquiries@kylebooks.com
www.kylebooks.co.uk

1 3 5 7 9 10 8 6 4 2

ISBN 978 0 85783 310 5

Editor: Judith Hannam
Designer: Nicky Barneby
Illustrator: Aitch
Production: Lisa Pinnell

A Cataloguing in Publication record for this title is available from the British Library.

Printed and bound in Slovenia by DZS Grafik d.o.o

CONTENTS

PROLOGUE

Would you like a neat and pretty garden: a rectangle of lawn, cheerful bedding, shrubs in decorative pots and a couple of deckchairs from which to admire them? Perhaps you already have an outdoor room: a haven, an oasis of tranquillity, dotted with dramatic low-maintenance plants, a gas-fired barbecue, cunning solar lighting. Does your small garden include a pond and a cut-flower patch? Is it measured in acres? Does it feature a pergola?

Then this, I fear, is not the book for you.

If, on the other hand, you nurse secret dreams of self-sufficiency, of orchards, livestock and *Little House on the Prairie*-style preserving, then come closer. If you are a frustrated enthusiast-in-waiting, with only a tiny growing space, or nothing at all; if gardens and gardening books intimidate you, or your only interest in plants is in eating them, you are not alone. This is my confession: my comically small town garden, a mere 6 square metres of urban soil and a few pots, is not a scented idyll of rambling wisteria in which to drink prosecco. It is a larder, in which I grow more than a hundred things to eat, including, in an ordinary year: eight types of tomato; five varieties of kale; golden raspberries; twenty kinds of lettuce, chicory and Asian greens; Italian climbing beans; about fifty herbs and a few flowers, all edible. I make salads with thirty different leaves; I harvest, by the teaspoonful, Juneberries, wild strawberries, tame strawberries, wineberries, loganberries, gooseberries, cherries, grapes, rhubarb, figs, quinces and every conceivable currant.

With variable success and modest yields, this minute area is a wildly uneconomical experiment in extreme allotmenteering: a city jungle, green and bountiful, combining edible cultivation with natural beauty but, sadly, nowhere to sit. Yes, I do mind that there is no space for a couple of small sheep but, despite this, it is a source of infinite happiness and deep peace. How could it not be? Taste this incredible shiso leaf. Listen to the hum of all those bees.

When visitors are shown it, they tend to laugh. It looks bonkers, yet I am in love with it. And, like all fools in love, I want to spread the joy.

Come into my garden. Try to keep a straight face.

LATE WINTER

'The garden was small, but intensely rich and
deep – one of those wells of verdure and fragrance
which everywhere sweeten the air of Paris
by wafts blown above old walls on quiet streets.'

Edith Wharton, 'Madame de Treymes'

OH DEAR

This is barely a garden. At its longest point, from the back door where we stand, towards the trellis at what I laughingly call the 'far end', it measures 36 . . . leagues? Not exactly. Metres? Try again.

No. We're talking feet. Its widest stretch, from one next-door neighbour to the other, is 25 foot, about 8 metres, no more. And it isn't even symmetrical. These terraced houses have brick extensions where once the outside toilet would have stood, so the shape is an almost-rectangle, missing its bottom right-hand corner. The surrounding walls are so dilapidated that snails cross long distances to spend their holidays in them, and eventually emigrate here, for a better life. The narrow area by the back door, the lower part of the not-rectangle, is paved; beyond the extension, where the garden opens out to its full width, the flooring is old red brick in a herringbone pattern, like primitive parquet. There is a 1.5-metre-deep border around this wider part, the three sections of which are known, imaginatively, as (on the left) 'the main bed', 'the bed at the end' and 'that other bit'. Yes, I am a novelist, and words are my craft.

So, 11 to 8 metres long, 8 to less than 4 metres wide, mostly paved; that is it. There is no grass. There is also no bench, pond, greenhouse, nursery bed, log pile, sundial, decking, terracing, pleaching, topiary, water butt, gate, wildflower meadow, nuttery, parterre, arbour, beehives, stream, rockery, gravel, climbing frame, hedgerow or hammock; no step or slope, no winding path. I own no potting shed or nesting box or wheelbarrow, no rake or strimmer, no polytunnel. Nothing like a fruit cage, or even a cloche. So how can I presume to write a book about my garden?

Usually, when writers talk about making a garden, they are describing the transformation of a wasteland. All my favourites began with sand or grass or naked soil. And however cramped Joy Larkcom, Eleanor Perényi, Mirabel Osler or Beth Chatto considered their terrain to be, their renovations always required stone to be removed and other stone brought in; barrow- if not lorry-loads of manure; native hedging bought by the gross and bulbs by the hundred; and trench-digging, weed-killing, stump-grinding, path-laying. Once everything was flat and windswept and now, look! A paradise.

Like meals, gardens produce great writing. Open Gertrude Jekyll or Elizabeth von Arnim and your mind will fill with fantasies of moist shade and lily ponds, aconites and bear's breeches, mixed borders, modest but important collections of epimediums. For practical advice and rampant fantasy, they are our allies. Whether we own a window box or an estate, each of us, when rootling about in the soil, experiences the same disappointments and unexpected pleasures, the secret laziness, the guilt, the balm to the soul.

Yet I rarely read them, these great garden writers.

It is not them; it's me. The moment they refer to the Lower Orchard, to stone benches or barns or fields or rills or, curses, manure heaps, my empathy dies. It isn't a world I recognise. It's the same with food. Banquets are fine, in their place, but wouldn't you prefer to read about midnight sandwiches and ingenious stews from kitchen cupboards, picnics on river banks, dinners provided by tiny Alpine restaurants during snowstorms? I don't want Christopher Lloyd's suggestion of tulips planted in 'lots of 12, 25 or 50' as a backdrop to one's swathes of home-bred wallflowers. I want to see, just once, in actual print, somebody admit to their lack of space for even one more seedling; to confess that, when at last they find a square centimetre of soil, it is invariably on top of a nameless allium bulb they planted the previous autumn, much too shallowly, with insufficient grit, and rather close to a horrible mauve geranium they bought from the garden-centre sale-shelf because they felt sorry for it.

Recently, books have been published for the modern urban gardener, whose acres are few. They lie. When writers and broadcasters refer familiarly to the constraints of small gardens – the fences, the narrowness, the cool dry shade – they are not to be trusted; turn to the photographs and you know you have been tricked. These people have space for verandas and high gates and fountains and statues and circular beds. Blackcurrant gluts! Box edging, damn them. That doesn't count.

If, however, you are truly desperate, with only a roof terrace or a balcony, yet foolishly determined to grow something to eat, there are a few books for you. They will promise miraculous yields from upside-down tomato plants, a year's worth of salads harvested from a compost-filled half-drainpipe. These, too, are false. They flagrantly ignore the fact that fruit- and vegetable-growing is extraordinarily labour-intensive, requiring so much more croon-ing attention than lawns or salvias. How many carrots will really grow in a self-watering plastic pot? If you want fresh vegetation but work full time, go down the market. Besides, who has space for 2 metres of horizontal piping?

Every year articles are written about office allotments; I believed them. Until recently I worked in an office where I kept a Red Cherry Hot chilli among the dictionaries. With weekly dressings of filter-coffee grounds and individual pinches of compost imported from Regent's Park it occasionally produced a couple of flowers, which I hand-pollinated. I would put the very occasional chillies it produced in my workbag, to bear home like a Nean-derthal with half a bison, only to find them weeks later, crushed beneath notebooks and coins like small unsuccessful fossils. But we were fighting a losing battle against fungus gnats and air-conditioning; like an ageing span-iel it clung to life but, when I heard myself asking my assistant to squash its aphids in my absence, I realised it was time to let it go.

I should have learned my lesson. But gardening had me in its silken grip, just as it has you. However unglamorous your plot or pot or shared allot-ment, however hopeless your harvest-festival dreams, once you have begun the long infatuation with soil and sappy green leaves, with shoots and earth-worms and the smell of rain, there is no rest. Yours may be a garden at which real gardeners would laugh. You may never have grown enough berries for a summer pudding, or successfully renovated a mature 'Rambling Rector' rose; neither have I. That is the point of this book. My garden is not a haze of cottagey colour. I don't have bowers of fluffy clematis or conical yew trees. There are no pre-planted pots of daffodils waiting to fill those troublesome gaps in my herbaceous borders, because I don't have herbaceous borders and I'm not sure I really like daffodils. But I am in love with the tiny patch of soil I do have, with the musky spice of tomato leaves and the flavour of a single home-grown raspberry. I am obsessed with the mere idea of buck's horn plantain and good King Henry, fiddlehead ferns and callaloo; with twining beans and courgette tendrils; the scent of leaf mould; the impossibility of gathering manure on busy A-roads; compost-making and germinating and my dream, if not actual ownership, of one perfect apple tree.

Gardening is not a hobby but a passion: a mess of excitement and compulsion and urgency and desire. Those who practice it are botanists, evangelists, freedom fighters, midwives and saboteurs; we kill; we bleed. No,

I can't drop everything to come in for dinner; it's a matter of life and death out here. Just give me another hour, or two.

CATALOGUES

When it's too cold and dreary to face the garden, and real life is not up to scratch, seed catalogues ought to provide comfort. This is, unfortunately, very far from the case.

'Picotee'. 'Naughty Marietta'. 'Slap 'n' Tickle'. 'Brazen Hussy'. Do these words thrill or nauseate? If the latter, come closer. Let us sharpen our secateurs with malice aforethought. Hell is stocked with libraries of unbearable works of literature, and gardening catalogues occupy a special place. Just as estate agents believe that 'impressive' is the highest compliment one can pay a house, suppliers of plants and seeds write of talking points, show pieces, drama. They seem to assume that our primary aim in growing flowers is to dazzle our neighbours: 'A semi-double bi-coloured parfait petite *with* ruffles, you say, Geoffrey? Really? Maybe I will stay for another drink.'

Like many writers, I find certain words excruciating. In childhood I begged family members not to say brisk, or pleasant, or cosy, or medley or moist. They ignored me and so my condition has worsened with age, like the English language ('veg', 'a bake', 'eat happy': these make me want to die). To the sensitive, garden centres are places of pain. There is already so much from which to avert one's gaze: die-cast piglets and repellently-scented candles and faux-stone boot-scrapers in the shapes of forest creatures; plastic mugs bearing odes to Nana; humorous peg bags; dyed potpourri; solar metal ducks; wood-effect LED lanterns; pink-flowered trowels for the ladies and Sneeboer Dutch transplanting spades for the rest of us. And if, when searching the seed racks, I spot a packet labelled 'Dwarf Twinkles', 'Merlin Morn', 'Zinderella', 'Teddy Bears', 'Boy O' Boy' or 'Spanish Dancer', I simply focus very hard on a good old-fashioned *Campanula rapunculoides* and the nausea passes.

However, navigating a cringeless path through catalogues is growing more difficult – or, perhaps, my sensitivity is increasing. Many of the more interesting seed suppliers insist on online ordering, ignoring the needs of gardeners who read in the bath, and forcing us to rely on the more old-fashioned catalogues, whose jargon runs the gamut from brain-shudderingly twee to simply absurd: 'eye-catching duplex lavender blooms'; 'collarette fleuroselect novelty'; 'showy but uniform'; 'a superb garden performer'. If people grow a sweet pea called 'Charlies Angels' [sic] or 'Knee Hi Mixed' or 'Karen Louise', how can they look it in the eye? I realise there is a limit to how often a copywriter can use 'orange' or 'short', but there is no excuse for 'be the first to grow these heavenly fragranced pastel hues for that something different'. Even fruit and vegetable suppliers, from whom one might have hoped for restraint, make horrific choices. Apples have famously beautiful names, like nineteenth-century courtesans – 'Beauty of Bath', 'Fenouillet de Ribours', 'Annie Elizabeth', 'Irish Peach' – so what barbarian could justify naming a potato 'Jazzy Salad' or a runner bean 'Lady Di'; sweetcorn 'Minipop' or tomatoes 'Craigella', cauliflower 'Candid Charm' or kohlrabi 'Korfu'?

There must be support groups; no one should have to deal with this alone. Perhaps we can petition seed suppliers to adopt some better names: 'Corduroy', 'Wuthering Heights', 'Aristotle', 'Metaphor', 'Sally Wainwright', 'Total Eclipse of the Heart'. I would happily advise them. Actually, I would pay.

RURAL LIFE

In one's twenties, gardens happen to other people.

We lived in a block of flats just south of Euston Station. We had forgotten about weather; mud did not exist. We bought our vegetables at Safeway and avoided the country as much as possible. Then, after our small scruffy car was broken into five times in a year, we moved out of the very centre of London, and understood what rural life was all about.

When it rained, actual snails crept over the pavements; cats and foxes roamed at night. The nearest green space was not a litter-spotted square but Hampstead Heath, big enough to get lost in. Our hair smelled of fresh air. We now occupied the top of a small terraced house, converted, by easily distracted amateurs, into a maisonette. Our downstairs neighbours complained about footsteps but look! Stairs! A roof! Never mind the damp and mice, the constant traffic jam outside, the rumbling trains, the merry drug dealers gathering outside the local school every time the lunch-break klaxon sounded. This was paradise.

Best of all, we had a roof terrace. It was edged with shoulder-height railings, and covered in fibrous tiles so leaky we had to mop it when it rained, like fire-watchers protecting St Paul's Cathedral. But we could see sky, and neighbours' sons shouting at the labradoodle, and something swishing in the wind that might have been an aspen. Downstairs owned the garden but pretty soon we wouldn't care; it would be the Hanging Gardens of North London out here. Just give me a couple of months.

And so, like a simple shepherdess, I skipped to my ruin. I bought two plastic pots, a sack of mud and a pair of purple clematises with Polish names, chosen in honour of my grandfather; I was returning to the soil. As every gardener knows, full-sized clematises are uniquely ill-suited to container growing; they need more water, deeper roots and room to roam. Understandably, mine died. I should have stopped right there.

Instead, I thought: blackberries! How difficult can they be?

This cycle could have continued indefinitely: a ceaseless tide of unsuitable plants – peonies, oak trees – massacred by exposure and poor research. But families grow, as do book collections; we needed children's rooms and, ideally, also a loft, a basement, a study each and an enormous dingly dell of a garden. Was that too much to ask?

Yes. Thirty-two houses later, each grimmer or less affordable than the last, we heard that the house directly opposite was for sale. Barely bigger than our flat, with a 1980s plastic kitchen and mouse-gnawed wiring, it seemed that impossible dream: a doer-upper. The only problem was the garden. I'd been looking forward to a hammock, fruit trees and, obviously, a lawn, but the estate agent referred only to a 'yard'. This sounded ominous. I squinted at the photograph: nothing but a shadowy tangle above paving stones, and not many of those. Where was the trout stream? Even a simple burbling brook?

Eight years later, I still remember the thrill as I forced open the kitchen door into the back garden. There was no grass; who cared, when around the prettily weathered brick and stone lay flower-beds: centimetres deep with real soil? There were trellises choked with roses and ivy, edged with terracotta pots, larger and older than I had imagined ever owning, containing a human-height rosemary and a bay, skilfully trained in the shape of a lollipop. Fat pigeons stood about on a somewhat lopsided fence. A mummy and daddy blackbird, whose song I recognised via The Beatles, hopped along a real brick wall. There was also an actual life-sized tree, rough-barked, miraculously scented, even in November. It was a garden, undeniably, and I wanted it. It was small, yes, but mature. *I* was mature.

Then we bought it, and the fun began.

The beds contained shrubbery; I knew that much. Further identification proved difficult. The photographs in my charity-shop *Complete Family Gardening Encyclopaedia* had faded to muddy magenta and bog-green, and the diagrams looked like physics exam questions but, at the back, before a list of recommended pesticides, lay a section on Fruit and Vegetables.

Life, for me, is an opportunity for eating. Interesting new foods are the purpose of every holiday; meals are what I want to read about in the bath, discuss with strangers and remember. So it is inevitable that, while most people think of gardens in terms of flowers, my instinct is always; 'What will there be to eat?'

I leafed through the disappointingly short chapter. Where were the dangling melons, the enormous tomato yields grown from one small pip? Under blackcurrants, it mentioned that 'nine or eleven bushes should be sufficient for an average family' and suggested that the adventurous try blueberries 'for a Transatlantic taste'. There was much discussion of exhibition-bench-worthy potato varieties, fruit-tree fertilisers ('Late Jan. apply sulphate of potash at $\frac{3}{4}$oz per square yard. Every three years, in late Jan., apply super-phosphate at 2oz per square yard. In late Feb., apply sulphate of ammonia at 1oz per square yard') and a sumptuous chart of diseases. It was, to be fair, an old and ugly book but in those days, before the publication of Nigel Slater's groundbreaking *Tender*, in which he listed individual varieties of lettuce and blackcurrant in terms of beauty, taste and growability, and Mark Diacono's brave, mad campaign to make gardeners think in terms of deliciousness, not tradition, even freshly published gardening titles focused on the old favourites: cabbages and leeks and pears.

This was not what I had imagined: not at all. Forget it, I told myself; *this* was my garden, shrubs and flowers, not an impossible utopia of almond blossom. I would concentrate on what already existed, chuck in a few bulbs and leave it at that. It was time to live in the moment, count my blessings and so forth. Time to get cracking; to garden.

But how do you garden with other people's plants?

HEDGEHOG NIGHTMARES

'Oh, roses!' said every visitor. 'How lovely!'

Idiots. Roses, particularly in a tiny garden, should be pretty and well-behaved; they also ought to keep their labels securely attached. Even I knew what a rose looked like but these nameless examples seemed more suited to fairy tales than to English gardens. Each was uniquely cursed. The one at the back, most visible from the kitchen, combined lovely glaucous slatey leaves with simple blossom in an appalling salmon pink. The second looked perfect, with sweet-scented cream flowers at the end of 3-metre shoots which waved ironically at me above the trellis, as their petals fell like manna on the slugs that grazed the bed beneath. And the third, scented, compact and beautiful, its blooms the colour of rhubarb fool, had stems like the stuff of baby hedgehogs' nightmares: mouldy, dappled, densely prickled.

If I was to improve them, I needed to know more. Were they large-flowered hybrid teas, cluster-flowered floribundas, modern bush or burnet or damask or gallica or species roses or simply shrubs? Did they ramble? Were they naturally bushy or in urgent need of haircuts and, if the latter, how did one go about this? And what about the other plants: this rubbery thing, this dusty sort-of-daisy? There were low weed-like leaves, and brown dead tendrils, and some buttercups. Is a shrub just a big plant, or somehow superior? Should one feed ivy and, if so, on what? The answer, surely, lay in books. Books made me; they are my favourite inanimate object, my salvation and, probably, my doom. They isolate and comfort, inform and distract; my childhood was built on them. Adulthood is unthinkable without them. And gardening, I swiftly realised, gave me an excuse to visit a whole new bookshop section.

I read my purchases thoroughly, their mysterious phrases soothing and exciting; then I brought them outside, ready to be informed. First was the leathery plant: a Portuguese spotted laurel, *Prunus lusitanica*. Apparently it reproduced sexually, contained cyanide and was 'long-lived', which seemed a pity. Next came a depressed smooth-leaved holly, or privet, then something which might, if it pulled through, become a cistus, and a plant like a fleshy rose whose prim sub-magenta blossoms turned to beige slime even before they fell. The solution, my book informed me, was to add acid to the soil, which was probably illegal and definitely stupid. Already, I knew more than a gardening manual. It was time to take charge.

I am not proud of the month that followed. I became like a bar-room drunk, trying to engage in conversation everyone who passed by: the butcher, veterinary nurses airing Schnauzers, Ted the boiler man. I would throw out leading comments, desperate for a fleeting mention of hanging baskets and then, if they strayed my way, I would pounce: 'Do you know what that's called? Is it a weed or do you like it? Do *I* like it? What is it for?'

I begged friends to bring knowledgeable relatives for tea and followed the only one I successfully lured, a surprised aunt, with a notebook which read afterwards like evidence for the prosecution: 'Sharp, get one. Ears?' A passer-by explained that the tangled flowers at the front, sweetly scented, 3 metres high and blossoming without pause, were merely an indoor jasmine grown feral, nourishing itself by sending its roots deep into the drains. We refused to believe her, although I wonder now if that explains the smell it emits when the blooms start to die, like day-old Chinese takeaway. We pressed on. By interrogating a probably harmless gentleman at a bus stop, I worked out that the tufty business occupying most of the main bed was crocosmia; one of the few benefits of my extraordinarily swotty childhood was that I could spot the dried remains of acanthus leaves, because the ancient Greeks carved them on the capitals of Corinthian columns. Everything else defeated me. I bought a soppy book on herbs and, ignoring the bath-infusion recipes, identified the tansy and soapwort and bugloss and dyer's aconite and enchanter's nightshade that lurked ominously beneath the shrubs, like an Elizabethan witch's secret store cupboard. There seemed to be very few recognisable flowers. It was lovely, restrained and totally alien. It made my fingers twitch. Yet, dimly, I sensed the need to wait. Even up here, kept warm by buildings and exhausts, I knew we were deep in winter. The garden was impossible to imagine in spring, let alone when ripe and richly overblown.

The answer, irritatingly, was patience. In my excitement I had already read enough to know what people do when they inherit a garden: they leave it for a year until, after flowering and dying back, the garden's bones (they always say 'bones') emerge. Fine. It couldn't be that hard. I'd just wait, and watch while, like the slow accretion of leaf mould, the perfect layout gradually formed in my mind. Then, armed with knowledge and a range of exciting tools, I would make my garden: painterly, old-fashioned, beautiful.

Oddly, that is not how it turned out.

HUMAN BLINKERS

In the houses of my childhood, kitchens were below ground level. If you wanted to visit the garden, even to pick a few chives (it was the Eighties), you had to climb up slippery outside steps. The basics of garden ownership, the sweeping and weeding, must have required an effort of will; if, every time one looks outside, one sees only a rainy stairwell littered with unswept leaves, it's tempting to stay indoors.

But this kitchen, my adult kitchen, is on the ground floor. You just open the back door and walk outside.

This is a nightmare. How am I supposed to resist the garden now? Although the door windows are modest, they offer a vista of paradise. Or, no, of something better: a paradise-in-waiting, needing me only to nip outside and perform a couple of simple tasks and then, definitely, it will reach perfection.

Making coffee lures me closer. Somebody needs to invent blinkers for humans. There are novels to write, tax receipts to collate, but where is the harm in standing at the glass for a little look? A light drizzle is usually falling; I am shoeless because I prefer to write in, although not with, bare feet. No sane person would step outside.

I step outside.

I blame my dyspraxia, recently diagnosed, by a friend, outside a pub. It explains many of my difficulties – with directions, practical tasks, walking through a door frame without banging a shoulder – in a way far more cheering than old-fashioned stupidity. I also tell myself it is the reason that I am strangely inattentive to cold. Unlike most British people, with our nice calibrations of weather, our conversational grumbling ('wet enough for you?')

and outrage at any climatic extreme, I don't pay attention to low temperatures. I feel them, obviously: I'm not a rock. I just don't remember to do anything about them. So while others would stop to shoe themselves appropriately before walking over grit or bramble or several centimetres of snow, I persist in believing I'll be able to tread lightly towards the compost bin, like a fairy o'er stepping stones.

'Where's your coat?' people ask. 'Aren't you freezing?'

'Yes,' I tell them, and we look at each other, perplexed.

Yet my plants are calling to me. From here I can see the garden table, which was bought for Mediterranean-style meals in the sun but mysteriously is covered in improvised plant crutches; broken teapots; ice-lolly-stick seedling markers; treats for compost worms; postman's rubber bands for attaching things; a child's stolen kitten-patterned pencil; takeaway cups labelled MANGO I THINK and ??MISC DON'T THROW OUT; stiffened gloves; rusty spoons. To a non-gardener, it looks like dismal rubbish. To me, it is a smorgasbord of delightful and necessary tasks.

Addicts are ingenious. They lie, even to themselves. A gardener can always think of an excuse to wander outside.

'I'll just . . .' we mumble. 'Give me a couple of minutes.'

This is obviously nonsense. How could one do anything in a garden in two minutes? It's like just one drink, one cigarette. A garden is a knotted rope along which small tasks and satisfactions are laid out at optimum intervals, as in a computer game, or a punishment devised on Mount Olympus to drive mortals mad. We try to resist; we fail. We always do.

'This won't take long,' we lie.

THE PERFECT GARDEN

Every garden needs a lawn. Even then, in the first seasons of my innocence, I knew that much. What else is there to do in childhood but lie, agonisingly bored, on unglamorous English turf? Childhood, particularly before the Internet was invented, is fantastically boring; if one is lucky, desperation leads one into the garden. On the extremely rare occasions when I wasn't reading, I could usually be found doing something peculiar outdoors: peeling sticky yew bark to make unsuccessful bows and arrows; fossil-hunting in the flower-beds; grinding bricks into paint; grubbing for earthworms, inspecting insects, listening to the melancholy coo of wood pigeons, contemplating the void. I tasted grass stems. I once attempted to cut the lawn with blunt-ended scissors.

So naturally I wanted my children to spend as much time being bored on a scrappy lawn as I had. The area in question was bedroom-sized, perhaps 4 metres square; all we needed was a couple of rolls of turf, turves. I had already bought a Swing ball. How hard could it be?

The first fourteen or fifteen visitors we consulted said we were unturfable, that no grass could survive beneath all that overhanging foliage. And where would we keep the lawnmower? People can be so negative. I wouldn't give up: what about running through sprinklers? Gazing at the clouds? We'd promised the guinea pigs; I'd whispered offers of lawn-grazing into their petal ears. They couldn't make do with carrot peel and stolen grass indefinitely. The books insisted on digging up the lovely bricks, and their foundations, adding 10 centimetres of topsoil, scarifying, seeding. In panic, I invested further: a hose reel, like a neon turtle; a wonderfully cheap shed, which went mouldy almost overnight; a set of inflatable goalposts. Slowly, I came to accept the inevitable: this would be a grassless garden. There was so much else to do – branches to prune off, fertiliser to chuck about – that sometimes I could almost forget my lawn sorrow. Almost, but not entirely; even now, when I catch sight of a particularly scrumptious patch of new spring grass, the urge to roll about on it, worry about the universe, get down on all fours and munch it, is difficult to resist.

So I began to consider my other options. Why had no one explained about all the rules? I learned that I should map my garden's hours of sunlight, but the sun never stayed out for long enough to be sure. Every child's gardening guide instructs one to test a) the soil's pH and b) its structure. Always the good daughter, I obeyed, as if I might confound expectations and discover an acidic heather bog under London topsoil. I tried to measure my soil's consistency; did a falling-apart sausage suggest that it was sticky or sandy? I borrowed a compass, and was wholly unable to understand which way the garden faced. I tried covering the graph paper with tracing paper, as if a change of stationery was all I needed. I attempted to measure my terrain in paces. I wondered where to put the pond. But it was only when I realised that a pond on this scale was essentially a puddle that I acknowledged my plans for a wildlife sanctuary, virtually a game reserve, would come to nothing. There would be no newts or tadpoles. No grass means no chickens. I consoled myself with thoughts of the inevitable slow-worms and grass snakes . . . oh, no, hang on. Not grass snakes. But surely rare spiders? Interesting bees?

We were, however, bountifully blessed with two animal varieties: cats and slugs.

The gardens of this terrace intersect, making a marvellous pedestrianised area in which dozens of felines, variously noisy, violent, randy and digestively vigorous, can perform their *passeggiata*. Our own rescue-cat, Hercules, is both saintly and handsome, unlike the creature with the irritating yowl, the weird pale stalker, the fluffy fat bully which harasses and mauls everything within a ten-garden radius. Their cats are almost as bad. If your flower-beds are a popular local toilet, no hoses or cayenne-sprinklings or rose thorns or unpleasantly scented coleus plants are going to deter them; no loans of fierce-looking dogs, no ultrasonic frequencies or even begging London Zoo for lion droppings – nothing works. Bulb planting and transplanting will be fraught with horror; unpleasant surprises lurk beneath every innocent snowdrop. I still run outside, barking; it makes no difference at all.

No true warrior surrenders. I had read that slugs and snails were the primary foe of gardeners but was confident that this would not apply to me. I bought lager, buried jars, strewed orange halves and waited. It was a major triumph. The bloated beery bodies, like exhausted darts players, were disgusting but endurable, because the garden was saved. My bloodlust sated, as a sort of victory lap I trotted back out to admire the baby parsley seedlings

I'd planted the day before. What foresight! What plantswomanship! Soon we'd be chomping on bunches of—

There was nothing. Every leaf and stem had been devoured by rampaging slug hordes, galloping across the plains while, like a fool, I slept. Slowly I understood the reason. The disintegrating walls of which I was so proud were a breeding ground, a sort of nursery, for the nation's molluscs. This level of slug infestation is rarely written about: most gardeners have enough garden to go round, or helpful toads or camera crews, or simply a free hand with the metaldehyde pellets. Whereas I, with my delicious tender salads and organic greens surrounded by untrammelled ivy and honeysuckle, had inadvertently created a slugs' hotel buffet; you could see them giggling and gesturing rudely as they queued for seconds.

Chastened, unbroken, I vowed not to rest until the garden was a fecund paradise, ingeniously protected from pests, dripping with ripe fruit, perfumed, inviting. How long could that take – perhaps a year?

It was an idiotic plan. It might just work. But troubles were coming, tiny ripples which turned to riptides. Life, the foe of peaceful gardening, intervened. A year, it turned out, was on the short side.

EARLY SPRING

'The cabbages were curled and purple and
full of raindrops, and their leaves creaked stiffly
as [she] held them in her arms.'

Elizabeth Taylor, *The Wedding Group*

BITTERNESS

In the olden days, maturity was easy to spot; if one could plough or kill or reproduce, childhood was over. In the modern era, we must look for more subtle signs. Have you ever driven through a car park with the parking voucher between your teeth? Do you appreciate Radio 4, and vests, and scenic mountain views? And, most tellingly of all, do you enjoy chicory?

Any fool can eat a carrot. Lettuce is hardly a challenge. Even kale, if sufficiently massaged and toasted and salted and covered in Parmesan, has lost its power to terrify. But bitterness is another matter. If salad leaves were cigarettes, lamb's lettuce would be menthol ultra-lights. And Gauloise? Gauloise would be radicchio.

Chicory and radicchio: are they the same, or almost? The world, particularly for gardeners, is already too full of interesting questions; we must prioritise. According to Joy Larkcom, author of *The Organic Salad Garden*, the latter is merely a red version of the former; let us accept that, and hurry away. But then there is frisée, the tougher curly form of endive; escarole, which is what Americans call green chicory; chicons, which require forcing … enough. We will focus on the Italians; life is better that way.

Italy is misunderstood. We think of it as a baking hot land of merry Southerners, frolicking in off-the-shoulder blousewear, but the reality is more temperate: mild springs, icy but manageable winters. Their tomatoes and sweet peppers and lettuce-leaved basil remain largely out of reach, but their salad leaves are within our pasty Northern grasp. Why accept a corner-shop iceberg lettuce or a soggy supermarket salad when you could try 'Variegata di Castelfranco', dramatically speckled with maroon, its pale jade outer leaves turning to lemony-white as you approach the heart yet remaining spotted and freckled with rusty red, like a murderer's comeuppance? I cannot get over 'Catalogna of Pugliese', continually drawing my guests' attention to its juicy dandelion-like serrated leaves, succulent buds and the occasional sky-blue flower right through the year and out again after a mild winter. I have an unrequited crush on the fat juicy crunch of puntarelle, which for three years I have tried to grow from an unpromising packet of seeds found on a nylon nightwear stall in a disappointing Piedmontese market. Better to stick to 'Grumolo Verde', the hardiest of all despite looking like a floppy green rose, or the Rossa di Chioggia types, their leaves wine-red, bright burgundy with minty-white ribs, or blackish-red and tightly packed as a tiny cabbage, torpedo-shaped or orchid-shaped or like a crunchy tennis ball. There is a gorgeous radicchio for all of us, each one multipurpose, extraordinarily brave in the face of disgusting weather conditions and delicious in almost every culinary context you can think of except, perhaps, blancmange.

Chicory has other uses, all of which I encourage you to ignore. Its roots do not make drinkable 'coffee', any more than it can confer invisibility, find treasure for gold prospectors or open locks. It is said to be a love potion and to strengthen the beaks of woodpeckers; I'm not joking. Proper gardeners scoff at such nonsense. They also force their best heads of radicchio, for paler, sweeter earlier leaves. Doesn't that defeat the purpose? Never mind the kiddies; wouldn't we adults prefer the brave taste of radicchio seasoned and dressed, for example, with oil and pomegranate molasses: salt and bitter and sweet and sour, all at once? Think of it in winter with walnuts, or blood orange, or feta or beetroot or maple syrup or, if you simply must have a green salad, I will go to a shop and buy you an ordinary lettuce, tear it up and mix it with these bitter beautiful leaves.

ORIGINS

There is nothing like the gentle lunacy of a traditional gardening magazine. With their regular sections on poultry-keeping and exhibition vegetables, their rotavator-care features, Wisley's latest scientific Brussels sprout trials and the delicious before-and-after photographs of Readers' Plots, with Swiss chalet-style sheds and floral displays in Wellington boots, they are as seasonally predictable as medieval Books of Hours, as expert as encyclopaediae. But these marvellous old-man magazines, even when they contain eight-page essays on soil remineralisation, are not quite enough. All of us, particularly at the start, need real-life examples, knowledgeable relatives, mothers with a mania for dead-heading and great-uncles devoted to their runner beans. Without them, gardening can seem a closed shop, accessible only if passed down by one's forebears, like congenital syphilis.

My path to garden enlightenment has been a lonely one, littered with money wasted and time misspent. When it comes to practical knowledge, I am self-taught, virtually raised by wolves because, selfishly, my grandparents failed to own cottage gardens. Instead they lived in small flats on big roads, whose noise and dirt and lung-crushing fumes were lightly sieved by net curtains and sooty geraniums, like a nourishing broth. At weekends, to show us nature, they'd dress us up like polar explorers and take us to Hyde Park, where we would manage six minutes of squirrel-hunting before hurrying back to the flat for squashed-fly biscuits. They wouldn't have known what to do with a hollyhock; in fact, their chief legacy was that, when I think of certain plant names, it is with a Hungarian accent: *MIM-o-so*; *FOOK-si-o*.

And so I have always felt guilty about my gardening obsession, like a white sport from a purple phlox: a strange, possibly disloyal, malfunction. Only recently have I realised that the passion may have been genetic. My mother's mother would storm up strangers' paths to rip boughs of blossom from their trees while her grandchildren cowered behind parked cars, pretending not to know her. She tended African violets and sansevieria, a Swiss cheese plant, a Christmas amaryllis in painted china pot-holders which we took to charity shops after she died, as all grandchildren do, and which now I long for.

My father's mother, widowed very young, very poor, never lived in a house, or rode a bicycle, or learned to swim. She once worked as a florist but her basement flat had little light in which to rear a child, let alone grow house plants. I suspect that this youthful vitamin D deficiency explains many things about my father. He is interested in everything: why not teach oneself Dutch or speed-reading or life-drawing? Why not make wine, or master real tennis, or wear a full-length, lemon-yellow, polyester, Senegalese kaftan to one's own sixtieth birthday party or, for that matter, walk to someone else's party dressed as a locust, in green man-leotard and sparkly tights? The man knows no shame. So, when he acquired a little house of his own in Oxford, modern yellow brick but with a grapevine growing up the side, he didn't think, as a sane person might have done, 'Oh, how lovely, I wonder when they'll ripen, though I don't know the variety, or understand bunch-thinning, or have a dead sheep with which to feed its roots, so I'll just pave it over, bung in a deckchair and ignore it for the next thirty years. We are, after all, in an alley by the Lamb and Flag pub, not the hills of Montepulciano.'

No: he had a much better idea. At the first whiff of summer he picked the grapes, piled them in a washing-up tub and added his precious daughters, me and my sister, instructing us to stamp on them with our plump pink bare feet. 'Come on!' he cried. 'Let's make wine!'

'No, Daddy. It hurts.'

'Don't be ridiculous! Stamp! It's fun!'

'But Daddy, it stings.'

'Get a move on' he bellowed and it was only when he noticed that we were weeping that we were freed. As you would expect, we remain traumatised by our acid bath, or pretend to be. He seems unashamed; in fact, he thinks there's nothing funnier.

Unwisely, we forgave him, and slowly further meagre scraps of natural history, other than 'avoid English grapes', also came our way. I suppose I should be grateful. He took us for walks in the park and showed us the sweetness at the base of dead-nettles and honeysuckle; he bought us Cox's Orange Pippins and shook them until the seeds rattled. He sniffed, unashamedly, roses and lilac. He grew small wormy pears, which he would ceremonially divide after dinner. He even experimented with courgettes, until my mother suggested that it would save time and money to have them individually flown in by private jet from Fortnum and Mason's, a hundred kilometres away. And now, although his era of vegetable-growing has passed, he has produced two townie daughters, both of whom are obsessed with their tiny gardens.

'I have something for you,' he announced when we visited last autumn. How exciting. Knowing him, the possibilities were limitless: a portrait in oils of his dog; extremely strong painkillers illegal in Britain; psychological advice in rhyming couplets; a wicker carpet-beater; four jars of mustard. I followed him into the kitchen. On the table lay a soiled carrier bag.

'It looks a bit . . . bloody,' I said. 'Are you sure?'

'It's grapes,' he said. 'They ripened.'

Pretending not to notice the smell of fermenting fruit, the luxuriant mould, I took it. I put one on my tongue: it was mostly pip, slightly aged, but tasted, definitely, of grape, of holidays and gardens, of his home-made mulberry gin and red grape juice at Passover and every glass of wine he had ever given me, of childhood.

'Delicious!' I said. 'Well done. You're virtually a farmer,' and, as I hugged him, I saw that he shone with pride.

THE GARDENER'S GAZE

Other people are so peculiar. You see them all the time, walking past their neighbours' front gardens, by great clouds of scented clematis or huge bosomy fragrant roses, and do they sniff? Even hesitate? Ripe blackberries may be lolling at them through the railings, bird cherries so close they have only to lift a hand, and they do not break step: not a nibble. I have never once spotted anybody ripping out the soft parts of horse-chestnut leaves to make fish bones or absent-mindedly putting a leaf of spicy wall-rocket in their mouths, before helplessly flapping their hands to cool the fire; or heard a grown woman being begged by her children not to dawdle on the way to school . . . except me.

It is mystifying. Nature is everywhere, in the playing fields we cross near the station, municipal flower-beds, tops of walls; why doesn't everyone want to taste and smell it, roll it in their fingers, ingest it, to keep them alive? This morning I put my hand in a jacket pocket and discovered four small borlotti beans, their plum-coloured dots and dashes still bright against creamy green; dried-up lavender stems; a few angular fragments of bay leaf; half a hazelnut shell; a three-holed flint a bit like an owl; and what I hope is a squashed nigella seed-pod. Yes, it's partly greed, of course; walks are much more interesting when one can nibble the sour fruity flesh of a fat vermillion *Rosa rugosa* hip, with its thrilling potential for death-by-fibres, or a couple of leaves of garlic mustard from the damp verge by the gate. But it's more than that. Those glimpses of green keep me going. And, while there isn't much to scavenge on freezing grey days, there's always a bare tree branch to stroke, or that ratty stand of pot plants outside the hardware shop which I look for every single time the bus turns right.

For those of us who think too much, self-reared in libraries, prone to fret, reading is salvation: a portable and side-effect-free analgesic. But even I can't read much when walking, so instead I admire the sorbus tree by the bus stop, inspect its label (*Hupeh Rowan, China*) and focus on its pinky-grey fruit, or touch a pussy willow catkin or the silken fleece of a *Stachys* lamb's ear, or even, if pushed, eat a daisy. It's not always easy. When your shopping bags are cutting off your circulation and the rain has turned to sleet, you don't want to start communing with a perfect Acer leaf. But there is greenery everywhere: beauteous, spirit-lifting and, best of all, edible. Even on the coldest day, a good hard look at the extraordinary leaves and stems of a tiny moss clod or a sniff of rosemary will give you a little strength.

Edith Wharton, twenty-nine when her first story, 'Mrs Manstey's View', was published, described the life of a lonely widow who lives for her glimpse of scruffy back yards: her greatest, indeed only, pleasure. It's a touching, if slightly clumsy, tragedy, with one remarkable feature: Wharton's precocious understanding of how the grottiest flower-bed and neglected tree can bring joy. Of course: she was a gardener in the making. Of the famous Italianate gardens she designed for The Mount, her house in Massachusetts, she said, 'Decidedly, I'm a better landscape gardener than novelist, and this place, every line of which is my own work, far surpasses *The House of Mirth*.'

Most of us would disagree; the gardens are a little grand, with their grass steps and Italian walled garden and rustic rock-pile fountain, but her fiction was great. If, in her twenties, she was noticing the 'hard white flowers' of a magnolia, the 'haze of boughs, leafless but swollen, which replaced the clear-cut tracery of winter', the signs were already there; here was the embryo, the cotyledon, of the woman who would one day produce both a great American garden and *Ethan Frome.*

Once gardening has you in its fragrant leafy grasp, there is comfort and interest everywhere. When you are tired or sad or cross, or, as so often, all three, it is still a pleasure to stand at a train window and see a flash of allotments, ingeniously terraced, tucked up in cardboard and black plastic, water-bottle cane-toppers swaying in the wind. There is also the pleasure of sitting in judgement. Despite the chaos of my own garden, I feel entirely justified in criticising everyone else's. How, I wonder, passing a front yard bigger than my entire growing space, could anyone actively choose rhododendrons? Their leaves could be cut from vinyl flooring; those wispy flowers are Pepto-Bismol pink. Was it really wise to clip that lavender quite so vigorously? Like the rest of Britain, I have fallen in love anew with dahlias but, good Lord, not with those ones, the size of a dinner plate in lemon-sherbet yellow. Is trailing ivy obligatory from window boxes? Is there ever an excuse for gerbera?

Yes, I may be horrifically ignorant, but that doesn't stop me disapproving. Hebes look like faded washing-up brushes; heather resemble dyed dried flowers; there's a house round the corner with hanging baskets and strawberry towers and an old-fashioned pram, packed with white and scarlet petunias and zonal geraniums the wrong side of smoked salmon. Their left-hand neighbours have slathered everything with dried-blood-coloured bark chippings; the right-hand garden is paved with what appear to be smokeless fire briquettes, leaving space for one anxious-looking rusty-red hydrangea, like something undergoing medical research. Using chillies as window-box fillers feels faintly immoral; are 'Numex Twilight' really meant to be that colour? Even worse are the low-maintenance bankers' gardens: regularly spaced heuchera, box balls and standard olives. They give me violent urges. I curse them with heuchera rust.

Nevertheless, there are consolations. Front gardens are ripe for camaraderie; no pensioner, gingerly lowering herself towards her primulas, is too unsmiling for me to attempt conversation, no foreign farmer too incomprehensible, once I've caught a glimpse of his elegant multi-stranded climbing-bean frame. Never mind that I have no idea what he's saying; we gardeners have a common language, comprised of enthusiasm, interest and a dash, just a soupçon, of entirely unfounded optimism.

WINTER WONDERLAND

All over the world, gardeners in early spring are united in a common lie. We pretend that we are prepared for the worst. We tell ourselves it doesn't matter, not much. And then we approach our favourite tender plants and peek inside their winter wrappings, braced for devastation.

We are talking about bubble wrap. The quince and fig and banana, the olive that fruits and the apricot that doesn't; the containers in which apparently hardy herbs, curly marjoram, stunted garlic chives, thyme and tarragon lie dead, or sleeping; the mildewed *Knautia* and slug-bedevilled pelargoniums; the unfortunate-looking loquat we reared from a seed (its dark lizardy leaves are large and stiffly ribbed as fans, with pale downy undersides to the pleats; its fruit, which is sharply delicious, only grows on other people's trees), the horseradish I keep out of loyalty to my sister, and the pomegranate, which was a stupid idea, are begging to emerge. My job is to resist their vegetable pleas. Frost could still strike. Do they think I spent hours devising them outfits from taped-together packaging materials and moth-wrecked blankets, just to watch them die? And what about the pots themselves, lying about their frost-repelling qualities, shedding terracotta shards like bits of piecrust? Some stand alone but the luckier ones are clumped together, wrapped like a German art installation.

In modern gardening, with our new love of tropical and architectural novelties, we often see treasured tree ferns swaddled in straw, or sacking, or even specially purchased horticultural fleece mob caps. Allotment owners use anything they can get their hands on: hay bales, home-made cloches built of coat-hangers and polythene. In allotments, make-do-and-mend eccentricity is a mark of commitment; it's perfectly normal to cover every centimetre in black bin-liners to warm the soil, or make a delicious soil-nourishing lasagne from cardboard freezer boxes, layered with carrot peelings, grass clippings and cowpats. It doesn't matter what it looks like, or smells like, when your plot is beside a railway track and everybody else is doing exactly the same.

But, for those of us whose garden is fully visible from the back door, packed with pots and tender fruit trees, our options come down to this: a winter wonderland of rotting snail-infested plastic rags, or annual plant death. Bubble wrap isn't pretty; a hundred separate shreds of it, stuck together with duct tape, are worse. I feel grateful and lucky to have a sort of home allotment, yet still envy owners of real ones, several rods' worth, some distance away from where they live, where they can buy cheap seeds and swap seedlings and help themselves to compost . . . let's be honest, I hate them.

Besides, every time we look outside there is the guilt: those plants we profess to love yet, because we ran out of materials, or started to shiver, or simply wanted a bath, we condemned to a winter of suffering. That poor unfavoured pineapple sage, which was still bravely producing its geranium-pink wattles in November: how could we not have wrapped it in something, anything? What about the picnic blanket; no one ever uses that. What kind of parents are we? Our punishment is to stand by the back door for another week or two, looking out, ashamed and fearful, as we await the Great Unwrapping.

There is consolation indoors: a little. Other people's generous sisters give them necklaces, or puppies; mine gave me a heated propagator. I had coveted one for years, telling myself it was the last thing I needed. I was wrong. It looks like nothing: a long shallow tray containing a carbon-fibre heating element, and seven small strong boxes, green below and clear above, with a tiny vent on top. So simple, but revolutionary: take, for example, the germination of tomato seeds. Until the arrival of this wonderful device, I grew them as follows:

1. Take one movingly furry-looking seed, either from a packet or, to make things a little more challenging, from a tomato you have enjoyed. If the latter, eat any remaining flesh, put seeds into well-washed marmalade jar, fill with warm water and a little washing-up liquid, leave for several days by the sink, to the disgust of family members, until the stink tells you that the germination-inhibiting jelly has been dissolved. Rinse seeds, dry on kitchen paper, cut out individual seeds stuck to paper and proceed. If the former, try to ignore the sneaking suspicion that you should have chosen a different variety altogether: the Russian 'Noire Charbonneuse', or 'Sungold F1', which always wins taste tests at tomato days. Where is the nearest tomato day? No, come back.

2. Fill small plastic pot with seed compost. Moisten rather heavily with contents of water glass still undrunk despite importance of staying hydrated. Insert seed.
3. Ineptly cover with a plastic freezer bag and elastic band, to form a little greenhouse; remember belatedly that something is needed to give height; remove plastic bag, insert wooden skewer on, then next to, seed; reattach plastic bag.
4. Place pot on already rather cluttered mat by back door.
5. Pluck ineffectually at plastic-bag covering as seedling germinates, in order to avoid contact between the two and subsequent rotting. Allow drops of condensation pleasingly to dampen soil, but wish had thought of stick or plastic spoon instead of sharp skewer, which is threatening greenhouse arrangement.
6. Repeat.

The propagator is so much more efficient. Actually, it's not, but it's more fun. The problem is that it's also dangerous. What is to control my untrammelled dreams of multiple chilli varieties now? No longer am I confined to garden-centre jalapeños: soon we will feast on Black Tongued Scorpions, Bulgarian Carrots, Carolina Reapers, Friar's Hats and Umbrellas and Hot Paper Lanterns, Grisù of Sardinia and Hungarian Black. Some are fruity, or good for drying in authentic-looking *ristra* garlands, or flange-shaped, or bred by Dr Fabián García at the New Mexico State University trials of which I have never heard but which must be important, and therefore desirable. I want them all. Technically, I could have them all. What was my sister thinking? I always knew she hated me.

Worse still, it's quite easy to balance the propagator on a tray on a chair on the mattress of the spare single bed in my study and then devote the day to rotating the little trays, watching as basil and Italian salad-seedlings crane their necks as the day progresses, only to have to crane them back when I turn them another 90 degrees. I may be pretending to write but really I'm watching my 'Green Zebra' tomato seeds germinate. Usually this room is freezing, by choice. Sometimes I think that this is all I need for fiction: a deep blue wall, an open window. The problem is that, thanks to the propagator, I can now also have seedlings slowly gaining strength at my elbow. Do they help me work? Of course not. They must be watered; I go in search of a cup and notice the green crime Penguins in need of shelving and the list of back exercises I meant to do every hour. I decide I want coffee, and, surprise, I find that I've drifted downstairs to the kitchen, to the back door, to the garden itself, wrapped and plasticky and still unbearably beautiful – anything, in fact, seems easier than sitting at my desk, making up stories.

WASTING MONEY WISELY

I have found my vocation: a Victorian parson. Provided that my bishop was relaxed about a few minor issues, I have what is surely the prerequisite of successful parsonhood: a mania for collecting. All I lack is the right equipment: soft badger-hair brushes and watchmaker's eyeglasses; lots of brass; walnut cabinets in which, labelled in florid yet controlled copperplate (I could learn, it's not too late), I can display interesting items: a belemnite, an allium head, a dead bumblebee.

What's that: dead bees and common fossils are hardly rarities? Nonsense. Think of the films you've seen and the novels you've read; are the objects in those cabinets truly precious, or is it the collecting that has made them so?

Rarity is exciting; of course it is. I am uncoolly proud of my fossils, keeping my section of ichthyosaur vertebra on a shelf for frequent gloating, and a small slab of ammonite bed within touching distance. But my desk is also littered, almost to the point of inaccessibility, with rounded sea pebbles, knots of driftwood, feathers and acorn cups and several vintages of conkers and a bird's nest in a clumsy Perspex box and shells and seed pods: always plenty of seeds.

Yes, it sounds silly. I am not a post-war schoolboy, nor a squirrel. But look, properly look, at the malty sheen of a new sweet chestnut, mahogany as a racehorse flank, or the frilly silliness of a nigella pod; the serrations on a pot-marigold seed; poppies' ridged rain-caps; the velvety secret inside a beech nut; the corduroy fluting of coriander seeds. Hold a fresh green teasel to your eye: see the hundreds of curved prickles which cover its surface, each varying minutely in length or angle from its neighbour like a flock of bird beaks, yet different again from the other spikes which dot its sepals and stalk. Admire the minute ridges on a stem of field garlic, carved with such apparent restraint, and their contrast to the stalk's curlicues. Appreciate the promise of those fat papery pips at the tip. Look, really make yourself look, at the infinite variety of stripes on an onion squash; lose yourself in fractals, thickenings and bristlings, the soothing repetition of perfect shapes. Photographs taken with electron microscopes have a thrilling weirdness; at that magnification, so has anything. The real magic lies in the seed or fruit of a flower or vegetable, even a weed, in the palm of one's hand.

Seed worship is a minority interest; for most people, beauty takes other, more sensible forms. It is the potential, the capability, of seeds that excites most of us and, sadly for me, I feel that as well. Seeds are heart-quickeningly addictive to buy: for half the price of a cup of coffee one can possess entire borders of sweet William, a meadow-full of campion and columbine, a twining riot of nasturtiums, morning glory, cup-and-saucer vine, *Rhodochiton* and *Thunbergia*; or, better still, tens of thousands of lettuce leaves, a potager in a packet, featuring varieties even the most specialist seedling-sellers can't match: 'Really Red Deer Tongue'; 'Fat Lazy Blonde'; 'Australian Yellowleaf', Italian 'Red Snake' and Austrian 'Speckled Trout'; bronze-tipped 'Marvel of Four Seasons'; 'Drunkard'; Reine des Glaces'.

Garden centres are torture. 'Hurry up!' we cry, performing hand-brake turns as we screech into the car park and leap out before the wheels have stopped. 'I'll just be a minute,' we say as, barging old ladies out of the way and mowing down weekenders, we're off to the display racks like a greyhound after a rabbit. It's a crack den in there; we may have sworn to be strong but, with one glimpse of a packet labelled 'rare' or 'good for bees' or, my own personal nemesis, Franchi, with its lavish seed counts, Italian glamour and gastronomic excitement, all is lost.

Our children and spouses know the signs; wearily they try to distract us, introduce reason, beg for a little self-control. Most addicts have been shamed by the blithe innocence of children; my own daughter was still in single figures when, having failed to divert me from a seed rack at Kew Gardens, she murmured, 'Well then, waste money wisely.' Our families know that we are already drowning in stale mixed-salad jumbo packs, that we hand out unopened envelopes of *Limnanthes* and Webb's Wonderful to chance acquaintances like an entrepreneurial dealer, yet cannot resist buying just one or two or ten packets more. They have witnessed the indecent excitement with which we try to set up seed exchanges; I love my sister dearly, but so much more when she brings her box of seeds to swap.

What they cannot know is our shame at the first glimmers of spring, the frantically nodding lone daffodils and recklessly blossoming lilac, the trace of life in the air. How can we confess to that sinking feeling: the knowledge that any minute now we will have to prise open our seed boxes and face, however privately, all those packets whose dates have now expired?

Seed mania is more powerful than regret, or reason. The most beautiful words in the English language are 'sorry, could we postpone our lunch?' but, when that miracle occurs, I don't spend my time exercising or making friends but engaged in disgusting acts of profligacy, loading my online trolley with imaginary harvests: yellow 'Bull's Horn' peppers, black-rooted scorzonera and pale salsify, Ceylon spinach, burdock, Spanish winter radishes. Usually, at the last possible pre-checkout moment, I manage to save myself, abandoning the lot just before reaching the till, leaving me financially unscathed but with a grubby onanistic feeling of vice succumbed to: my seedy shame.

Is it the names which are so compelling: flowering purple choy sum, lady's bedstraw, agrimony? Or the suggestion that one's world might change if one buys *this* packet, its contents lovelier, both more delicious and slower to bolt than any seen before? My desk is heaped with notes to myself about the latest pressing need: today's is the wild carrot, *Daucus carota* 'Dara', good for hoverflies, pinkly creamy as raspberry ripple, the mere idea of which makes my skin itch with desire. In the same way that sellers of anti-ageing creams and Japanese ceramic sushi knives feed off our dreams of a better self, so too each packet of seed seems to promise brave new worlds of horticultural triumph. Cupcakes I can refuse; I have never yet played poker, nor taken crystal meth. Yet however many packets I already have in my enormous seed box, if you offer me an ancient kale variety, a rare Serbian bean, a bee-magnetising Korean mint or, let's be frank, a 39-pence packet of radish seeds from my local pound shop, I am lost.

There's something else, more illogical still. Annuals grown from seed are cheap and varied, but also the greatest waste of time and space one can imagine. I work; I have a family; yet, at the first whiff of spring, I spend my few moments of leisure sprinkling seeds on compost, balancing improvised plant pots on roasting tins, bringing them out for a gasp of fresh air and then back before nightfall to harden off their milky stems. Have you tried the Japanese method of repeatedly brushing seedlings with the side of your hand, while grating cheese and phoning the dentist? I certainly have, and I don't even own the correct brush for it: not yet. I also have no greenhouse, nor even a deep windowsill; this house was built by barbarians. The seed trays huddle in the kitchen, defenceless against the assaults of footballs, brooms, wrestling teenagers and interested cats. Even the cheapness is questionable; for the price of a tiny bag of vermiculite I could fill the garden with ready-grown cabbage plug plants, reared by professionals, toughened by the winds that race across the Norfolk fens. Yet I persist, raising tiny quantities of flea-beetle-bitten leaves, doggedly, by hand.

In this era of hipster artisan craftiness, we all know that home-made is inherently satisfying; that slow, thoughtful creativity is a source of joy. But salad plants are not marmalade. Your specific requirements (sugar-darkness, shred-thickness, novelty citrus choice) may force you to make your own, and it may well be better than any from a supermarket. But there is nothing inherently superior about a home-grown 'Little Gem' seedling. So why do it? Puritanism? Penitence for buying too many seeds in the first place?

Yes, all of these things and a desire for quiet. It should be possible to chat while organising seeds, yet invariably I become distracted, trying to remember if there's something waiting to germinate in this takeaway espresso cup so carefully packed with compost, or if that old plum stone has sentimental value, while my conversational partner pauses, falls silent, abandons me altogether. So it's usually alone, at the kitchen table, when the house is quiet, that I sit, pretending I am performing a boring duty but intensely happy.

I have now bitten the bullet and looked at last year's seeds. My darlings live in a colossal wooden crate, ungainly to lift and horrible to carry, precariously packed with a range of chocolate boxes, biscuit tins and one of those uselessly tiny vintage-style 'My Seeds' canisters sold by manufacturers who have no idea what they are dealing with. Seasonally I subdivide them: in a plastic bag I've stuffed every packet relevant to the next couple of months, the tomatoes and chillies I have already cursed by planting too soon, the rocket and chicories and lettuces which in a few weeks will kick off spring, if only I can wait that long.

DRY STONE WALLS

Designing a garden is not difficult. One simply needs to draw it to scale, working out the horizontal baseline, the boundaries and trees (using triangulation) and, with a compass, offsetting all the beds and paths, assessing the aspect, areas of shade and exposure and, obviously, correlating it with photographs, before adding one's planting plan, bearing in mind the height and depth of each plant in relation to the whole. Anyone with the least recollection of school geometry and basic common sense can do it.

I am, sadly, not that person. In daily life, I struggle. Do you, on holiday, find you can sense your way through unfamiliar alleyways? I get lost in rental apartments. At home, I always head out of shops in the wrong direction, invariably confuse left and right, am mystified by even the simplest diagram and, much like a Tibetan Living Buddha, often find myself surrounded by a delighted audience which greets with laughter and amazement my attempts to assemble or repair even the simplest objects. Like my father before me, I am devoid of the slightest practical ability, the least sense of how I and my surroundings fit together.

But come now. Bit of graph paper, a tape measure: I couldn't let this defeat me. I started on the bed at the end and immediately discovered a problem. The stupid tape measure was too short! Without somebody to hold down the end, or a really enormous piece of chalk, it was impossible to work out the garden's length: ridiculous. No wonder Britain's manufacturing industry is in such bad shape with tools as poor as these. I struggled. I stretched. Do you realise quite how athletic, even in a small garden – no, particularly in a small garden – one has to be? Everything is so tightly packed, so wobbly and awkwardly balanced, that simply reaching a wall requires balletic *jetés* and *pas de chats*, and planting a bulb involves tiptoeing across whatever tiles and pebbles you have remembered to put on the already overcrowded soil, grasping tilting bamboo canes and flimsy tendrils like a brave explorer crossing a ravine.

Further difficulties emerged. The first hurdle over which I tripped, then fell, was how to relate a paper plan to a three-dimensional space, that is, the garden. The relevant parts of my brain seemed not to be there. I re-checked my favourite garden plans in Joy Larkcom's *Creative Vegetable Gardening*, but the photographs seemed unrelated to the diagrams; where in real life were these neat circles of artichokes? Was this even the front? Plans of beautiful gardens, their raspberry patches and sprawling courgettes reduced to geometric shapes, are meaningless if one finds weather vanes a mystery and always assumes that one is facing north.

With difficulty, I accepted my limitations. I must be an artist, not an architect; I would abandon theory, the bourgeois conventions of line and form, and paint with plants alone. Yet, for an artist, wasn't I strangely under-interested in how the garden looked? Oughtn't I to be highlighting the verti-cals, planning cool borders and swathes of autumn tones, instead of wanting only to get down on all fours and stroke, sniff, taste, rootle around in the soil and feel for the fat shells of tulip leaves, the gentle prongs of snowdrops? Would I still count as a gardener if I ignored contrasting secondary colours?

And what of the earth itself? As I crumbled and dug and measured, I chanced to notice that the beds looked a bit, well, flat. Shouldn't I enhance them, so everything would grow? No matter that it was still early spring, frosty and dark. The answer, as everyone knows, was manure.

Have you seen the price of excrement in central London? When I was growing up, the people next door kept a horse in their ordinary-sized shed; we could hear it neighing as we ate our chicken Kievs. Nowadays the only horses I see are solemnly clip-clopping through the quieter streets of Marylebone, on their way to anti-austerity marches; too massive-flanked, too stampy and policey to approach with a carrier bag. So much unused horse poo; it's mad-dening. I recently read an article on Humanure. It is only a matter of time.

Are there other sources? Lee, owner of Truffles deli round the corner, used to work in the Household Cavalry Mounted Regiment and I think he misses it; at Christmas he dresses in a top hat and drives a horse-drawn car-riage which one can hire to amuse visiting relatives. I am not yet quite far gone enough to scoop up the squashed droppings in the street, but I can't help thinking that Lee, so intelligent, so informed about salami and coffee, is missing a trick. Never mind the wet walnuts; might not a sack of manure be kept at the back, for special customers? Lord knows, I would take the lot.

Is there really nowhere else? The nearest city farm, where I have admired frogspawn and gingerly patted sheep with a thousand other guilty urban parents, gives it away; then one needs to let it rot in a heap for a good six months. I would love to have the space for a mound of reeking faeces; who wouldn't? But my family, unfairly, already object to the foetid comfrey feed, buckets of stagnant rainwater and rotting pondweed with which the garden is littered. So at ruinous cost I bought two sacks from a garden centre, invested in seaweed meal and ground pumice and something called Soil Improver, spread it thinly on the beds and waited for crops.

However; there is always a However. The borders were marginally higher than the central area, loosely edged with a single layer of uncemented bricks. When it began to rain, and did not stop, my expensive enhancements were first moistened, then diluted, then washed out of the borders and into the middle, creating a convenient reservoir of nitrogen-enriched slurry. I tried moving the bricks closer together, beginning a hellish cycle of repositioning. I tried plugging the gaps with small pebbles which worked as well as you can imagine, or slightly worse. Something more permanent was needed.

New railway sleepers seemed expensive, for logs; old ones would be more romantic but what of the toxins left over from the chemically reckless days of British Rail? Besides, how was one meant to manoeuvre them into something resembling raised beds? Gardeners seem to divide into those with staff, those with husbands and those with naturally occurring Do It Yourself skills. If I paid someone to haul in the sleepers, I'd still have no idea how they should arrange them. I looked into alternatives, all disappointing: rolls of split pretend-logs and picket fencing from the pound shop; kits of racing-green plastic edging with ingenious fixings which, even apart from their hideousness, would prove unimaginably complex for a mind like mine.

It rained on and on; my own private natural disaster continued. Then I had a brilliant idea.

This garden has no leeway: no neglected outbuildings, no bits of pretty willow fencing forgotten by a previous owner. It did, however, have a small pile of bricks, probably left over from the herringboning some years before. Might a miniature wall, two or even three bricks high, work? Perhaps. I tried this at the far end but the result was wobbly and wonky; it wouldn't do. Somewhere I'd read about bricks at an angle, forming a small dogtooth wall a good 15 centimetres high. No need for cement, or expertise; I had no one to advise or warn me. Full of the courage of the stupid, I dived in.

Two days later, the main bed had an edge. It was, and eight years later remains, magnificent, a sort of metropolitan dry-stone-walling, my pride tempered only by the fact that the soil level is now several centimetres higher than the brick tips, and the bricks themselves bulge outwards, like Olympic weightlifters just before they drop the dumbbells. The bed at the end still has its pathetic double-brick horizontal barrier, in whose many gaps an unending army of slugs muster, protected from all weathers, hugging themselves with their non-existent arms in delight at this crèche, this drop-in centre, this home I have made. And the Other Bit? Nothing but the single brick-height border it was born with, over which the soil washes freely, down to the clay beneath.

With precocious wisdom, I decided to concentrate my efforts on the main bed and face the others later. But, before it could fulfil its destiny, changes needed to be made. The Portuguese laurel and the rotting rose still occupied a good third of that bed's area and, even in my ignorance, I sensed that cabbages and so forth would suffer in their shade. At last I had a use for our saw: a Woolworth's Junior model, costing £1.95. It served me well. Next came the cistus, which was mostly dead already, brown and rustly as dried flowers in a tea room. Boldly I grasped its dry branches; the whole thing came out in my hand. And now I couldn't stop; to make space I seized upon another little shrub, never identified, whose sulphuric greeny-yellow lit up the corner opposite the kitchen door and which I regret losing, or rather killing, to this day. I uprooted what might have been hellebores, attacked a buddleia, cleverly pruning all its lower branches so that only the top, far above my head, could flower. I dug out what seemed to be diseased bulbs but, in retrospect, were the corms of the handsome scarlet crocosmia. So many leaves and stems and branches, so much wood; it took days to chop it up for removal, together with part of my knee. Then the house's former owner came to visit.

'How,' she asked, 'is my camellia?'

'Ah,' I said.

HOW TO TORTURE
A GARDENER

1. Send her to stay in a vast and intriguing house set among world-famous kitchen gardens, extraordinary fruit trees, ancient oaks, lavish Victorian greenhouses and a shop.
2. Keep her indoors.

I am only here to be friendly. We have come to West Dean College, a famous centre for arts and crafts, on a short woodwork course: a birthday present for my partner, who once passingly mentioned a desire to build a bookshelf. Friends laugh at the mere idea of us in a workshop; I fear they are right. My plan is to avoid the saws, perhaps try nailing a few planks together and then leave her to it, all keen with her apron and sharp pencils, while I roam the grounds having creative thoughts.

We arrive at night, on the bus, gusts of rainy wind prickling our faces as we trudge to the entrance in our silly London clothes. Several courses are running simultaneously; our fellow students are mostly semi-retired and wearing gilets; they are here for tassel-making, enamelling bowls, Intensive Mosaic and weaving life-sized willow stags. There is a polite sign begging visitors not to pour hot chocolate in the water fountain. At dinner (curry, mashed potato, chocolate sponge) our tutor warns us that the weekend's project, an oak step-stool, will fill every available scrap of time: after meals, early morning.

This is a terrible mistake.

By Saturday lunchtime (fish pie, boiled carrots, syrup pudding) we are on the verge of signing up for next September's course (a portable bookcase). West Dean is paradise. Power tools are marvellous. I have tucked a pencil behind my ear. Chisels, you say? Mortice joints? A ferocious electric band-saw for carving ogees in our stool-sides and a punch-drill for whacking two penny-sized holes for the handle? Let me at them. Everything is difficult by any standards, let alone for a spatially challenged innocent who can't be bothered to measure, yet, thanks to an exceptionally helpful tutor and extensive wood-glue, progress is starting to be made.

But I must see the garden. Even more pressingly, I must visit the shop.

'Do I have time?' I ask Mark, the tutor, who combines the appearance of a cynical Rockabilly with the patience of a well-paid nursemaid at a Swiss spa.

'No,' he says.

'Please?'

'No.'

'Please. I'll plane really quickly.'

'No.'

'I am desperate.'

'You are mad,' he says. 'Enjoy your run.'

The receptionist does not understand that I need instructions but no, I don't have time for the arboretum. I can't read maps; please, I beg, just point. The grounds of West Dean are enormous, stuffed with flinty buildings and pottery studios; totem poles, steaming chimneys and temptingly closed gates; an unappreciated 4-metre galvanised water trough which I consider stealing; a pergola of famous length which, in winter, looks as uninviting as a shed snakeskin. Snowdrops and daffodils and crocuses sprinkle the wet grass; they have planted and naturalised 500,000 beside paths and trees, like drifts of surprising autumn leaves. By the time I glimpse the tables of burgundy-streaked hellebores outside the shop, their heads waggling in the wind and rain, I'm almost running. Please, I think, let there be seeds.

Also, please not.

I am in luck, arguably. No seeds, no books, but plenty of miniature pewter trowels and handmade buttons. All compulsive seed buyers know the relief one feels when spared a binge, the downside of that dopamine high. I hurry out to inspect the scanty display of early spring plants; fortunately, none of them is edible.

Meanwhile, in the workshop, everyone else will have aligned their mortices with the tenons and be chiselling away extraneous timber, while I'm roaming the gravel paths, fondling pine cones. This is ridiculous; there is not time to visit a single plant; besides, my teeth are chattering. I canter through a gate and find a fruit garden, deserted. The grass is too soggy to cross; there is no blossom, not even the merest suggestion of a fruit but, oh, the espaliering. Some have been trained into multiply-layered conical pyramids like Lego trees; others as rococo goblets, the stem squat and ancient, the spurred verticals like fingers tied to their cages. They are closer to taxidermy than horticulture, or the nasty beauty of lizard skeletons. At this distance the smart metal labels all seem to say 'Pear'; the fans trained on the outer wall could be anything: sour cherries or peaches, obvious to anyone who could work out whether it faces north or south but not to me.

I pretend to myself that the way back involves the greenhouses.

The first door I choose is a mistake: warmth, ferns, ripened gourds. I have no time for such fripperies. The second is emptier, full of drying bamboo canes. But the third is packed with dozens of variably sized terracotta pots, each containing the most expertly grown salads I have ever seen: cress 'Bubbles', winter purslane, 'Red Russian' kale and 'Jagollo Nero', purple mustard, chervil. These are the aristocrats of winter vegetables, weed-free, plump and frisky. Furtively, I taste them all; they taste, in truth, no better than my own pasty and dissolute seedlings, but they look dazzling.

I am late back to the workshop; my colleagues have already begun to saw through the tops of their Miller dowels. My only triumph is that I have bought nothing but, for the rest of the day, I am unable to stop thinking of the apple blossom in spring, the berries in summer, apricots ripe for purloining, sea kale to shoulder height. I need to come back, have time to see the gardens in all their glory. Could one perhaps spend extra not to do a course?

WHAT WENT WRONG

I was showing a visitor round the garden. It didn't take long.
'Lovely,' she murmured. 'So jungly. So green! But . . .'
'What?'
'Do you not like flowers?'
An awkward pause. 'Why?' I asked.

'It's just that some people *do* grow vegetables . . . but not usually in the town.'

I didn't mean to become an edible gardener. One minute I had acquired a garden full of happy shrubbery and ardent ground cover, easy to tend, a pleasure to look upon; a few months later I was tearing most of it out and, despite total ignorance, laboriously raising from seed dozens of things

I wanted to eat. Gradually, grudgingly, I'm beginning to see how odd this is. Admittedly, I have little interest in anything non-edible; I also have a worrying penchant for trying to eat everything anyway (twigs, paper, raw root vegetables, orange pith, children). However, there is such a thing as balance. A reasonable person might ease themselves in gently with a pot of basil. Then, if their enthusiasm developed, and I think we have established that in my case it probably would, they could move on to a few peas in a single large container, perhaps a blueberry bush, a row of carrots. They might be tempted by one of those terrifying family apple trees advertised in colour supplements, in which several varieties are grafted onto one poor rootstock, but probably would stop there.

And why would any novice gardener stray from the path of Traditional British Produce? Of course I tried to grow it, because that is what one does; I'm not an anarchist. But could I honestly tell the difference between my 'Pink Fir Apple' and 'Arran Pilot' potatoes and a kilo of supermarket 'Maris Pipers'? The broad beans were ravaged by black fly, the garlic bulbs barely exceeded the size of the original cloves and, in order to reach anything like normal size, the handsome 'January King' cabbages each required twenty-four-hour slug patrol, seaweed granules, blood, fish and bone, nematodes and a couple of sweeps of a treacle-covered card with which to catch flea-beetle, while occupying half a square metre of soil for eight months, nine months, ten. By the time they reached maturity, their outer leaves snaily and yellowing, their hearts marked with the unmistakeable navy-blue Morse code of caterpillar poo, it was difficult to feign enthusiasm.

Slowly I came to wonder: was there any point in laboriously growing tiny crops of easily bought food? Most British gardeners, tiptoeing shyly towards growing edible plants, are programmed to experiment with root vegetables. They can't help it; it is hard to forget the allotments of one's youth. However, thanks to my foreign grandparents, I had reached adulthood with neither nostalgia nor disgust for any crops in particular. Unscrewing my stabiliser wheels, I cut loose my anchor and rode off, alone, into the wild.

Never mix metaphors. Out there, alone and unguided, the mistakes were tragic. The expense was terrifying. I should have stopped there but when have common sense and passion ever mixed? I want to grow interesting fruit and vegetables well but also yearn for variety: the more romantically foreign or historically vivid or delicious the better. If one prefers a crunchy lettuce leaf, why wouldn't one be curious about 'Red Cos' or 'Rouge d'Hiver'? Everything sounds better in French; before one knows it, one is being led like a child through the woods towards other glamorous-sounding options, 'Rouge Grenobloise' or 'En Cornet de Bordeaux' and then beyond, to, for example, winter purslane, which saved Californian gold-miners from scurvy, or red-veined dandelion, so charmingly called *pissenlit* by the French. If one sows a salad mix, generally combinations of rocket, mizuna and the utterly pointless lamb's lettuce, isn't one then tempted to grow more of the highlights? That's how I discovered 'Red Russian' kale, the tenderest and prettiest brassica of them all: in a pack of the upsettingly named 'Frilly Gourmet'. Even before I first gorged myself on Joy Larkcom's *Oriental Vegetables*, a sachet of Spicy Mix had lured me with its siren cry: try 'Green in Snow', it crooned to me. Mmm, look, mibuna. Shungiku. Kai-laan. Kai-laaaaaan!

HELP ME

It is time for the annual catastrophe. I have sorted my seed packets, ordered a few more and then others, and still others; don't tell me it is nonsensical to buy extra, for the free postage. I am too busy for such petty concerns. Yet I am worried. What if my *cime di rapa* seeds fail to germinate, like last year's batch; wasn't this the same packet? Wouldn't it be wonderful to have some professionally grown spinach, or reliable parsley seedlings, or, hold me, a grafted aubergine? Isn't buying in seedlings the sensible, no, the *economical* solution to my unusual needs?

So I saddle up the laptop and am lured to disaster. Just as supermarkets are planned by dark masters of shopping, tempting us to buy cereal bars and DVDs when we only needed milk, Delfland Organic Plants is designed to destroy me. Would it be better to choose the Brassica Selection, or the Small Chilli pack, or a pick-and-mix combination of everything? I need a Basil Collection. And, unfortunately, 'Nine Headed Bird' Mustard Greens from the Real Seed Catalogue and six tomato plantlets from Simpson's Seeds, although that would barely scratch the surface of my increasingly uncontrollable desire, not to mention golden bush courgettes and miniature cucumbers and, while I'm at it, isn't it logical to change my fairly arbitrary choices to non-F1s so I can save their seeds, then add a few packets of F1 seeds, 'Sungold' and 'Dasher', as well?

So, naturally, I order all those and, in the infinite wasteland between purchase and arrival, a few extra flower seeds and also three canes of yet another raspberry. The plantlets arrive when I am out; I return after nightfall from a long day twice in a row and, on the third morning, I force myself outside to face them, lined up like fragile underage recruits, too dry, too cold, to survive another hour. Of course I'll find room for them. How hard can it be?

THE GETTING OF WISDOM

Books are always enough, except in the garden.

The best ones rarely make it outside. They are rumpled by bathwater, taken to bed to lull us with descriptions of aged pear trees, perennial skirret on Welsh mountainsides, tiny wooden bridges in Chinese citrus orchards built to make life easier for predatory ants. But, like all enthusiasts, we also yearn for fellowship: to marvel at the triumphs, to laugh at the disasters, to give advice, to, forgive me, share. Isn't this part of the pleasure? Taste this, we urge. Smell these. I know it's funny-looking but, please, try it. For me.

Young people don't garden. In their twenties they experiment with recreational drugs and inexpertly mixed vodka cocktails; thirty somethings spend their weekends at spinning classes in neon leggings, or discovering the café society of Bruges, not stratifying catmint seeds. When this madness began, my friends all lived in flats; flower-beds were something their middle-aged neighbours tended. But I was born middle-aged and, having acquired a hobby, I needed company.

In the city, one gardens alone. Villagers know each other's business, neighbours in suburbs keep an eye on each other's hydrangeas; in their absence, might an allotment be the answer? I would be surrounded by gruff but kindly pensioners, on hand to identify weeds and pass on some of the unwanted rhubarb with which, I had read, they were overrun. Even one would do; I could swap light manual labour for olde vegetable lore.

Unfortunately, the allotment lists were already filled with urban clichés like me, desperate to grow amusing squashes; I would be a pensioner myself before a plot came up.

To my peers, I was in the grip of an embarrassing infatuation; older people smiled at my callow enthusiasm and then edged away. There is a limit to how much one can glean from a chat on the bus. Yet gardening has limitless joys and the one I discovered next is this: that moment when the spark catches, when you realise that an acquaintance nurses the same frantic passion, and your friendship bursts into life.

Pat lived quite close by; she was much older than me but very beautiful, with a terrifying telephone manner. Just after we moved in she rang: 'I'm coming to dinner.'

'Oh! Golly!' (I never say golly.) 'Are you? When? Maybe Thurs—'

But she had hung up.

She brought the dinner: a slab of sea trout, a version of Jane Grigson's Sauce Bercy with tarragon and a carrier bag stuffed with leaves.

'This is what?' I asked.

'Salad.'

'I have some.'

'From a shop?'

'Well, yes.'

'Don't be ridiculous' and, just like that, my life changed track.

My growing interest in plants was worrying me; did it mean I was already over the hill? Was the next step a fleece and a sensible haircut? But, as well as sharp secateurs and firm opinions, Pat had sex appeal. If she gardened, it was safe, even advisable, to do so. She offered me a baby fig tree: easy, pleasurable, like a gateway drug. I visited her garden; she gave me a Japanese wineberry, which I immediately killed; then wild garlic, in a Victorian pot ('Don't return it, I have thousands') and tomato seedlings: 'Peacevine Cherry', 'Broad Ripple Yellow Currant' and 'Tiger Tom', their labels written in indelible ink.

A fortnight later, she stood at my front door. She was wearing perfectly tailored, tan, Italian military trousers with zips at the ankle; a blue cashmere cardigan.

'What a *sweet* little garden,' she said.

She had come to check that I was removing the tomatoes' side shoots. I was not; life had intervened, leaving me too feeble to do anything but sit, but I felt too shy to explain. She did it for me, then tied them in properly with beautiful tarry-scented twine, plainly disappointed in her young pupil. Later, on the phone, I told her the truth.

There was no limit to her knowledge and guidance, her generosity; and then there was. The last time I saw her, a few months later, I was stronger but she was in hospital. She, too, had had a secret; by now it was too late. I brought her a tiny autumn salad from my garden: sorrel, savory, sweet cicely, Malabar spinach, baby Russian kale and Chinese chives. She managed half.

I never saw her again.

MID SPRING

'Spring is sprung
De grass is riz
I wonder where de boidies is?
De boid is on de wing
But dat's absoid
I always toight
De wing was on de boid.'

Anonymous

LET'S GET HORTICULTURAL

The soil is warming. We gardeners grow ever more watchful, sniffing the air as excitedly as beagles, peering into the vegetation to detect those first thrilling signs of life. Is that a distant haze of green? Wait: did you hear birdsong? At long long last, after months of enforced dormancy, the suppression of our hopes and dreams, we tell ourselves that it might be time to begin.

It isn't time. Control yourself. This year's inevitable freak weather conditions will mean that there are still several degrees to go before sowing in what is hilariously called open ground, but is one seriously meant to test it by sitting on the beds naked-bottomed, as, in the Olden Days, gardeners were alleged to do? I'm not convinced. Did grandes dames settle like hens among their riding skirts to assess the soil? Were under-gardeners in stately homes instructed to sit in rows, warming the herbaceous borders with their skinny haunches?

My neighbours have seen too much nightwear-based gardening already. I keep myself indoors, focusing my energies instead on sowing extra coriander (its fresh green seeds last year were so delicious), forcing myself not to begin the heat-loving flowers, zinnia and tithonia, and checking my seed trays for daily, if not hourly, proof of life. Sap may not technically be rising but spring is in the air, breaking out all over; the patches of blue sky, the whiffs of chlorophyll and damp fertile earth. At the first bright morning, the touch of sunlight unfurling our shoulder muscles, we are drawn irresistibly outside. Others will comment on the beauty of spring, the chirruping of birds and scudding clouds; we are on our hands and knees, crumbling up soil clods and investigating rotten roots, absurdly happy.

Very few writers have admitted this, except for my beloved, Karel Čapek, the Czech author who invented the word 'robot' and, after becoming the Gestapo's Public Enemy Number Two, died in 1938 of double pneumonia and a broken heart. In *The Gardener's Year*, Čapek reveals the gardener's secret: paeonies may bloom, the sun may shine, but we barely notice. We would much rather have our bottoms in the air and noses to the ground, occupied with the part of our gardens we truly love: the soil.

If, Čapek wrote, a gardener entered the Garden of Eden, 'he would forget to eat the fruit of the tree of knowledge ... he would rather look round to see how he could manage to take away from the Lord some barrow-loads of the paradisiac soil ... "Where are you, Adam?" the Lord would say. "In a moment," the gardener would shout over his shoulder; "I am busy.", Čapek also suggested that gardeners evolve into invertebrates, to save the wear on our spines. Nobody else knows about *The Gardener's Year*; please read it. You will smile at every page.

Spring is the most over-described season. While we wait, agonised with impatience, to sow seed and move plants and generally run riot in the adult soft-play area that is our garden, we all need something to calm our nerves. Some turn to alcohol, or energetic exercise; the swottier among us start reciting poetry under our breath. I have two favourites: A. E. Houseman's 'Loveliest of trees the cherry now, something about fifty score, tum tum ... to see the cherry hung with snow' and the rather more infantile poem, read in a children's book of comic verse and never forgotten, with which this chapter begins. One recites it in a cod-gangster accent; I don't know why. Spring is a mystery.

ANGST

This house is on a notoriously busy city street, surrounded by roaring traffic; we are blanketed daily by a fresh coating of frightening emissions, our windows peppered with black dust, our lungs flailing in a fog of diesel fumes. Can home-grown really be better when it's perfumed with exhaust, grown on several centuries' worth of clinker and coal and household filth, nourished with ever more complex poisons? Why buy organic vegetables yet grow one's own mostly on bought compost made of who-knows-what, fed with oil-slick-polluted seaweed meal and, in convenient pellet form, the ground-up excreta of battery hens and the bones of miserable cattle?

Who am I kidding? My harvest isn't pure. I'm killing us all.

Most of our striving for health is rotten with compromise. How many factory processes were needed to make those delicious quinoa-based toddler snacks? Which is worse: chemically ripened hydroponic tomatoes or no tomatoes at all? Even the most obsessed gardener knows that there is more in this world to worry about than contaminants on one's home-grown perpetual spinach. Yet, if organically inclined, the thought of all those carcinogens and heavy metals, petrochemicals in the plastic containers and creosote in railway-sleeper beds, is an infinite source of worry.

For some, the solution is permaculture. I believe in the horticultural aspects of permaculture; I just can't face vegan cheese, wind dancing, poetry recitals in living willow bowers, rhizome flour, squalor, freezing well-water, children in bamboo nappies called Thames and Luna, soap substitutes, carob and pregnant women boiling millet while their stoned menfolk discuss the I Ching. One sniff of a joss stick and I start ranting about compulsory Latin; this is not a world for me.

The alternative is to stick to growing flowers. The city is plainly not farm-land, I am clearly out of my depth and flowers are pretty, cheering, good for bees and nobody laughs at them. Why coax this blighted soil to produce things to eat?

In explanation I offer the words of a security guard at the British Library, where this book was written. Think about it: it is spring. How am I supposed to work at home, when my study is a cold, bare, dusty cell and outside all is fecund, verdant, sexily shimmering with hints of sunshine, sniffs of rain, living, frisky soil? Would you expect an alcoholic to write about gin within easy reach of the drinks cabinet?

So there I am in the only place I can be trusted not to garden: the Humanities One reading room, waiting for the guard to check my bag. All I know about this guard is that he is Afghan, which doesn't lend itself to small talk. Unlike his cheery colleagues with their V-necks, he has always seemed forbidding: shaved head, black beard, mirrored aviator glasses, like a bodyguard. As he searches my muddle of notes and gardening books and seed catalogues for contraband, I hold my breath. Then he gives a mighty grin and says:

'Veg-et-ab-les, huh? The best thing in human life.'

The British have never been obsessed with growing food. Unlike our Mediterranean cousins, who cram tomatoes and vines into courtyards and allow lemons to drop all over their drives, here we grow flowers for decoration and buy our food from shops. Money permitting, why would anyone choose a handful of unripe gooseberries over a supermarket tropical fruit salad? Those who, for reasons of sentiment or health or inclination, do cultivate things to eat, tend to think of them as unconnected to the beauty of trees and flowers. We hide our efforts in a patch at the far end of the lawn, or stick thyme and parsley in a window box, water them copiously and watch them die, or ignore the couple of warty apple trees at the end of the garden because we feel guilty, or, if we are serious, rent an allotment and grow potatoes out there. Gardens are places of leisure and beauty. Food is another matter entirely. Isn't it?

But edible gardens can be beautiful. Just as a great French potager is part of the glory of château gardens, a tiny kitchen garden can contain just as much texture and movement and variety as the conventional lawn plus flowers, as many shades and tones and infinite beauty. Some have taken this principle further. The books of Rosemary Verey and Joy Larkcom make designing a truly ravishing herb and vegetable garden, tightly plotted, wantonly decorative, seem possible, even realistic, provided that one is the sort of person who plants leeks in rows and trains pears into goblets and has the discipline not to mix one's lettuce but to plant them in colour-contrasted blocks, green and red, smooth and serrated, in a pattern worthy of the Château de Villandry.

There is another way. The reason I love Joy Larkcom so is not that she elevated vegetable formality to art but that her *Creative Vegetable Gardening* also dared to show how a cottage garden, a jumble of fruit and flowers and vegetables and herbs, could be beautiful too. She opened my eyes to the possibility of wild strawberries as ground cover and arches of pumpkins, fennel for height, honeysuckle entwined with squash tendrils, great trembling pyramids of bean flowers and the murky gloss of 'Bull's Blood' beetroot leaves glistening in late-afternoon sunlight. Yes, I breathed as I looked through its pages, that is what I want. A symmetrical grid of raised beds, full of orange 'Indian Prince' pot marigold and raspberry-pink rhubarb; beefy red cabbage splayed under furry red wineberry stems; lipstick and tangerine and golden rainbow chard, snowy dame's rocket and sweet peas for the pollinators, dripping strings of 'Red Lake' currants, cosmos and lemon thyme, perhaps a 'Munstead Wood' rose providing a luscious damson backdrop to clumps of miraculously unflopped garlic stems. A little formality: a neat border of yew or step-over apples, with a riot of hollyhocks and courgettes behind.

But, much like Ahab's dreams of Moby-Dick, my great vision evaded me. There was less flaying and melting of blubber, not nearly as much harpooning but, I like to think, we shared the same doomed intensity of purpose. We both knew exactly what the ideal looked like. Obtaining it was more complicated.

I still know how my garden should be, yet, as always, enthusiasm has led to chaos. I am distracted by the silver mercury drop of rain at the golden throat of an emerging 'Prinses Irene' tulip and forget I came out here to restake the fallen blackberry 'Waldo'. Sacks of potting compost and council bags and watering cans must be within reach, which hardly makes for an elegant view from the back door. My brassica mania means that I grow too much greenery and not enough colour. Perennial kale is magnificent only above knee height, but the slug plague means that its stubby bare shins can't be disguised with chicories and lettuces. And this lack of decorative saladry ensures that however many gooseberries and garlic chives I plant in the main bed, interwoven with wild strawberries and the odd resentfully purchased but secretly admired pollinator attractor, a tiny red clover, achillea and sedums, the soil is still mainly bare compost, knobbly with eggshell fragments and half-composted nectarine stones.

Never mind all that. Look at the scarlet and lime baby leaves of spinach; the tight neat rosettes of golden marjoram, miraculous survivor of the frosts. Prettiness is always out of reach, but beauty? Everywhere: look around you.

VERTICALITY

Perhaps it would all seem better if I had a tree.

Trees make a garden. It must be true; I saw it on television. Books and websites and magazines insist upon it; even the most understanding modern writers bang on about Japanese cherry trees and paperbark maples, as if every single reader must have a decent-sized lawn with a neat circular bed just waiting for a good perpendicular. Without an illusion-creating, space-expanding, eye-muscle-stretching vertical, we might as well give up. When in the mid-Sixties Christopher Lloyd, the Mae West of gardeners, wrote a book called *Shrubs and Trees for Small Gardens*, he didn't mean gardens like mine; this book, he explained, was for owners of 'gardens of no more than an acre'. I checked: an acre is approximately the size of a football pitch, which means little to me. Calculated backwards, however, I've established that my garden is 0.0015 of an acre. I wish I didn't know this.

But what of the rest of us? Trees need roots; roots need soil. If our soil is packed into containers, or ferociously squidged between toppling bean pyramids and gouty sprouting broccoli, what then?

There are always trees in pots; I don't believe in them. It's like foot-binding one's children: a valid space-saving solution but morally tricky. Besides, if the trees are to fruit, the balance of food and water is almost impossible to perfect and there is a limit to the purely decorative value of a spindly leaning 'Cambridge Gage' tree, as I know from sad personal experience. Neither my costly dwarf apricot nor my autumn raspberries have produced so much as a blossom. It's very embarrassing. The only successes I've had so far are with a dwarf quince, a 'Lescovac', which last year produced perfect pearl-pink simple blossom, although admittedly no fruit; a pound-shop morello cherry which throws out branches like an excitable hedge; and my fig from Pat, because figs, unlike children, appreciate a spot of root restriction. Their combined harvests could be counted on, indeed fit into, one hand.

You may say I should have fed them, or kept them warmer; oh, I did. They just weren't interested. And so, like a disenchanted cult member, I am beginning to accept an unpleasant truth. Those photographs of 'patio' dwarfing fruit trees which pretend that eighteen apricots could easily grow on a miniature shrublet, aren't strictly accurate. The 'Mirabelle' plums and 'Black Worcester' cooking pears about which famous chefs rhapsodise grow elsewhere, on real trees, not on a stunted poxy freak squashed into a lily pot by the compost bin. Fruit trees in pots are an affront to nature. We have been conned, or allowed to hope, which is worse; can we please now have an amnesty and confess, for the sake of the easily led, that a container-based garden will not keep us supplied with fruit for a single day?

Yet those dreams of semi-self-sufficiency refuse to die. I can't stop thinking about apples. Just as Mme Bollinger drank champagne – 'I drink it when I'm happy and when I'm sad. Sometimes, I drink it when I'm alone. When I have company I consider it obligatory. I trifle with it if I'm not hungry and drink it if I am; otherwise I never touch it – unless I'm thirsty' – I eat apples whenever possible; cooked or raw, dried or puréed, right through the core and on to the stalk. Really I should have a nosebag – four or five a day is nothing. Think of how many a horse might eat, then double it. I'm on my third russet right now.

So, naturally, I decided to grow them. My expectations were modest; one or two trees should be enough. Already I pictured the rosy fruits, the delicious baking: oh, I'd say, casually, that's a 'Howland Wonder'. Just give me a season, I thought, and I would at last attain my deepest yearning: an apple-storage rack.

Well-grown interesting apple trees are an investment, difficult to justify when one has, for example, a family to feed. I chose my first, a 'James Grieve', because I'd tried it once, in childhood and, like a little weirdo, I vowed one day to grow my own. Yet, even after a lifetime's planning and careful saving, like most owners of a brand new baby I was totally unprepared. Stuck in the corner, admired but untended, it was quickly overridden with woolly aphid: adorable puffs of lamb's wool which, when you touch them, coat your fingers in bloody-black insect corpses.

Second victim: 'Charles Ross', an allegedly handsome dual-purpose apple, bought in an act of madness. The year had begun badly and quickly grown worse; it suddenly seemed a brilliant idea to start training fruit trees in espaliers against our neighbour's extension. A pre-espaliered tree was expensive; doing it oneself involves a simple twice-yearly process of shortening the main central leader, the side-branch leaders to the third tier and the laterals, and spurring back and tying into the appropriate wires, thus maximising yield-for-space and looking fantastic. Why didn't everyone espalier? Really, people are so disappointing.

The sapling arrived tagged like a plucky evacuee, with clear instructions about removing its straw and hessian packaging and planting it *immediately*. No, quicker than that. But I was in no state to plant it and, with packed lunches to make and children to dress, no one had time to faff around with trees. It leaned patiently by the back door in its sacking shroud, pining for the spacious orchard it might have known, had its life worked out differently.

When other gardeners complain of lack of space for a tree, they don't generally end up paying Darren the washing-machine man to crowbar up a paving slab. The ground beneath was largely builders' sand; I scooped it out while, behind me, the poor sapling keened to itself, contemplating its fate.

By now, it was night of the fourth day; it was looking very thirsty. Even I, killer of seedlings, sawer-down of healthy camellias, could not allow an apple tree to die of disorganisation. I unwrapped it, then discovered that I had no John Innes no. 3, no manure, no home compost in which to plant it. Into the hole went a horrible mess of seed compost, coir and peelings, and then the 'Charles Ross'. Give it a few days to settle in, I thought, and then the pruning of side-branch leaders could begin.

Poor tree. Do you know how long it takes well-supervised apprentices to learn how to espalier? Or how high slugs can climb? Or how dry semi-dwarfing rootstocks become if they are planted in the shelter of overgrown walls? I did not. I couldn't even remember which rootstock I'd bought: was it M9 (limited) or MM106 (semi-dwarfing somewhat vigorous for poor soils)? Was it even a 'Charles Ross', or had I made that up? It did its stunted best, for a year, then, slowly, centimetre by centimetre, like a leper, died.

Third victim: an 'Orleans Reinette', a birthday present. Because it was pot-confined I overindulged it, feeding and tending it like a prep-school milksop. In its fourth year, it cropped, triumphantly; the apple was small and tasted not noticeably different to any other apple I had tried. Last autumn, its fifth, its yield increased by 300 per cent. I'd had high hopes for this year, was already looking forward to the wrapping and storing my glut would require and so, a moment ago, stepped outside to admire it and discovered its bark scored and scraped as if it had strayed into the path of a roadside hedge-cutter. I suspect our cat, Hercules, working out his troubled childhood. The poor tree is for it.

And yet, to my fury, we do have a proper tree, occupying a full square metre of open soil. It is a scented viburnum, tucked into the corner by the shed, its multiple rough stems making access to the compost bins perilous and painful, its twigs entangling themselves in my hair like a passionate octopus. My unique pruning style has left it narrow yet tall but it cannot be shortened, because its most, indeed only, attractive feature is the compli-cated maze of branches, faintly Japanese if you squint, outside the bathroom window. It is a good 5 metres high; think of its appetite. And, in return for draining the moisture and minerals from more deserving life forms, the comfrey and rhubarb and the sorry-looking sarcococca, it produces dull leaves like needlecord and matted clumps of baby-pink and brown blossom; sweet-smelling, yes, like strong honey, but to what purpose? None of it is edible. I resent it more with every wasted season. Its days are numbered, albeit quite high numbers; it is the most successful plant here by some way, so arboricide needs careful thought.

If one isn't meticulous, a garden this size can look like an infant's activity blanket. Height must be obtained somehow, even by sneaky means. My kale grows tall, if unappetising; the banana, whose mother last year produced a huge succulent flower, golden-yellow and fronded like a sea anemone, has leaves 1.5 metres high. It isn't enough. I want a whispering copse of white filbert hazels, or at least a pecan. In the meantime, I am creative: very.

The poor bamboo canes bear the brunt of my mania for construction. I am constantly lashing them inexpertly together to form structures which wobble and list. One is meant to overwinter them somewhere dry, in the capacious and watertight shed that ours, recently named Barry, fails to be. Instead, possibly because I resent the canes for not being beautiful and traditional hand-coppiced hazel, I leave them recklessly in the soil through snow and rain, expecting them to multitask as cat-deterrents, crutches for recumbent purple-sprouting broccoli or disintegrating bean teepees; being a bad craftsperson, once I've produced something even faintly stable I'm too smug to demolish it. By the spring they look like bedraggled military banners, entwined with dead nasturtiums and withered leaves but they draw the eye upward, if only to the thicket of ivy on the wall above, clinging on like a comedy beard. Besides, I tell myself; it's nearly time to plant this year's batch of 'Cosse Violette'. Is it really worth taking them down?

Cities must have monuments: Big Ben, the Chrysler Building. Gardens, as any fool knows, need a focal point: an ancestral *faux bois* stone trough planted with hothouse-reared *Arctotis* × *hybrida* 'Mahogany' will do fine. Sadly, this garden's visual epicentre, its Eiffel Tower, is a solid wooden washing-line post, 10 centimetres square, bang in the middle of the outlook from the back door. This year, I promise myself every year, I will cloak it with something uncompromisingly decorative, sweet peas or a passion flower, yet, every year, I laboriously construct my terrible bamboo erections for the beans while the post stays nude and proud.

This washing post compels me. I can't sling up a swing from its boughs or pick its apples but, like a puzzled Caliban, I keep leaving offerings at its feet, or foot. Peculiar branches lean against it looking, I hope, like sculpture, although on reflection they're more like the skeleton of a bonfire, a place to burn martyrs. Unusual logs, mostly stolen, lie beneath it, waiting to interest wildlife. Shouldn't one only scavenge when one has space for the results? Luckily I don't live by the sea; the driftwood, the mysterious grilles and tools and glass would drive me mad with desire. We aren't all Derek Jarman; one minute you've found a lovely rusty hook and the next you are the star of an extreme hoarding documentary.

If I need to look up, I have to go elsewhere. Salvation lies eight minutes' walk away, through quiet streets lined with predictable gardens: *Verbena bonariensis*, unobjectionable white tulips in season, endless leathery *Clematis armandii* and far too many smoke trees, *Cotinus coggygria*, whose best feature is their other name, the wig bush. It's all horrifically tasteful. When one arrives at the heath, one exhales.

The heath is wild, for London; at least, that's what we tell ourselves. This is a beautiful illusion. The fallen trees rotting like bull elephants shot by poachers, the dark groves of beeches and uncountable nests and dens and hides, rely on tactful management, without which it would be a maze of bramble and fern: no paths, no grass, no vistas. My family thinks of its secret places as ours, as does everyone else. In a good year, it keeps us in blackberry crumbles. Even in a bad, when all one can find is tannic, half-rotted bobbles, already fly-blown and seedy, there is always something to bring home: a long strip of plane bark, holed like cartoon cheese; a bleached twig, a thin cross-section of branch. I prop up what I can on the bookshelves but the big ones, the corkers, go into the garden beneath the washing post, as if, with enough encouragement, a woodland will grow.

THE PATH OF
MOST RESISTANCE

It takes time to understand that the secret to edible gardening on a miniature scale is small, intense tastes. You can buy celery from the corner shop, bake a nameless potato: nobody will care. What will transform your soup or sandwich is two or twelve or a couple of dozen interesting extras: sorrel, lemon verbena, orange thyme, Greek basil, Japanese bunching onions, red oak leaf lettuce and green and pink Mexican tree spinach, cream-streaked mint and the pink buds of society garlic, black cherry tomatoes, bronze fennel fronds, purple hyssop flowers and sky-blue borage. The joy a white Alexandria strawberry will bring, the satisfaction in a quince you have hand-reared like an orphaned kitten, is immeasurable. You can buy almost anything, except pride.

The truth is that I seem to grow nothing normal. Broad beans are sweetly delicious if eaten very fresh, but there will never be enough. In a small space one can produce a handful, maybe two; still chewing, one looks sadly at their stems, knowing they are over for the year. Was all that effort, the slug-battling and tying and protecting, worth it? Ordinary green beans are impossible to spot late after work, in the dark, with a torch; leeks are useful but take up space. That, at least, is my excuse. So instead I grow purple and yellow and curly Italian beans; Egyptian walking onions and Babington's leek, *Allium ampeloprasum* var. *babingtonii,* instead of the perfectly normal 'Bedfordshire Champion' onion; New Zealand spinach, not the Popeye kind; green and yellow tomatoes and golden raspberries. And, of course, being rare, these mostly have to be grown from seed.

This is a fairly substantial downside. There are others. Cussedness is the less attractive sibling of stubbornness: sullener, more prone to being teased. No normal child, after several years of piano lessons during which they have neither learned to read music nor attempted Grade One, decides to learn the French horn, the most difficult instrument in the orchestra. No sane teenager, if such a thing exists, voluntarily reads the minor works of famous novelists: Thackeray's *Henry Esmond*, Dickens's *Barnaby Rudge*, George Eliot's *Scenes of Clerical Life*. You will be surprised to learn that that child was me. And so, when I say that I needed to cover a wall, your expectations may, justifiably, be lowered. Rather than choose something obvious at a garden centre, such as a *Clematis* 'Bill Mackenzie' in full flower, I was thrilled to discover the existence of *Holboellia coriacea*, the Chinese sausage vine, which has uninteresting leaves like bay, but without its scent, or usefulness. Its fruits, however, claimed its seller, a fellow lover of edible perennials, are delicious. Why would he lie?

So I brought it home, proud to be once again that rare gardener who dares to try something different; not for me the humdrum pyracantha, a glory vine, predictable old Californian lilac, with its fussy waxen leaves and flowers like inter-dental brushes. I was a plant collector, virtually a pioneer. Yet, when I reached for my more esoteric gardening books, looking forward to having my excellent judgement confirmed, I found no mention of it. Every other imaginable plant seemed to be featured; the books extolled bulrush-seed flour and the unconvincingly named breadroot and pickled elder shoots and argued, almost convincingly, for filling pillows with the hairs of the fruits of the reedmace, *Typha latifolia*, yet the sausage-vine was ignored. At last, I found it online; it clearly almost never fruits and, if it does, they are 'good for stuffing'.

Obviously I *want* to grow good old-fashioned 'Royal Sovereign' strawberries, with a century of happy market-gardeners behind them, but how could I have resisted buying a chokeberry, *Aronia × prunifolia* 'Nero', with its romantic Native American history? And then of course I realised it needed a mate, for pollination, but somehow ended up with an edible blue honeysuckle, *Lonicera caerulea*, instead. Over and over again, the susceptible will make the same mistake, until they have, as I do, a garden of young, unpollinated one-offs, solitary reminders of the puddings that might have been.

Why are edibles so exciting, the rarer the better? What Mirabel Osler called 'the perversity of rareness' is fascinatingly under-examined; psychologists believe that the desire to collect comes from our anxiety about death, or our search for comfort, or an evolutionary urge to gather resources in order to attract a mate. I know only that it is compulsive; that, once the bug has bitten, the unusual becomes an end in itself.

I've never found a 'Whinham's Industry' gooseberry for sale: very productive, with red hairy fruits, it sounds adorable, the perfect variety for me. In its absence, I am a martyr to every alternative that crosses my path. 'Tell me honestly,' I beg the stall-holder with a Bhutanese gooseberry, *Ribes griffithii*, 'how much worse is it compared to a normal gooseberry?' and, only if he admits that it is truly terrible, its yield pathetic compared to my existing 'Careless', even more likely to be sawfly-ravished than my 'Hinnomaki Red', will I be safe. The back of my diary bristles with agonised Post-its saying, 'Oca? Yacon? WHICH?' or *Rubus nepalensis*: vital'. You could tell me traffic lights produce edible husks and I'd be eyeing them up at roadsides, wondering how to drag one home.

I'm not yet so far gone that ease and yield have ceased to matter. It is the thought of a less obvious but better plant, more fruitful and delicious, which drives me. Who would not want that? But the least reference to a promising edible sets me a-quiver. It is, let's be honest, a sickness: unfortunately for me, a pleasurable one. As others desire pornography or 1950s Leicas, my pulse quickens at my favourite plant list: 'Norwegian Melancholy Thistle: our collection from a moist ditch near Tromso, Norway. Robust and very attractive to butterflies and bumblebees' or 'an unusually curly mint' or 'Japanese Plum Yew: edible sweet drupes'.

BARK

Then there are the freaks that live among us, like unicorns pretending to be ponies. Take the silver birch: not a domestic beast. My parents' garden is dominated by one, a bulbous monster whose pretty yellow leaves and round catkin-scales rained upon us throughout childhood; I still find them in my paperbacks. My father announced recently that the tree surgeon had visited, yet no one has mentioned the tree's mysterious affliction: multi-stemmed buboes on its trunk. Browsing through an oddly translated field guide to Danish plants in a second-hand bookshop, I spotted a reference to the fungus *Taphrina insititiae*, which causes 'witches' brooms' to sprout. Might this be it? Is it curable? I want to ask my parents, but they would take it personally.

At thirteen I climbed this very tree, with my friend Lisa. She was much braver than me; her parents were divorced and her mother's garden contained ferocious geese whose large green droppings looked like paint and smelled like blue cheese. With only a long cotton strap of mysterious origin we hauled ourselves incredibly, astonishingly high; I clearly remember reaching the level of my sister's bedroom, which is on the second floor. I can only hope that I have made this up. Lisa now works as an A&E doctor in Aberdeen; we have lost touch.

Silver birches are the trees of fairy tales and mountain forests; they are magical, so we want a piece of them. Passing schoolchildren tear their bark right down to the lower layer, the pinkly tender-looking periderm; we adults must resist this. Our reward is being able to admire the uppermost layer in stripes too high for them to reach: the grey-green lichen, the pale scales. The shreds curl the wrong way in one's hand, revealing the beautiful rusty underside untouched by the oval lenticels which spot the layer beneath it like secret scars. But it is the strange pale layer of bark below which is so exciting: that moonlit whiteness gleaming, like a gift. Of course I peeled some; it has dried in my pocket into a rustling crust, the lower layers stained reddish, the upper translucently frail as drying seaweed. I have a lovely Russian tea caddy constructed of suede-soft birch bark, stamped with what appears to be a tomato-vine motif; maybe, I mused, I could make something myself; absent-minded as ever, I put a piece of bark in my mouth.

I have always imagined that my love for these ghostly trees comes from my Eastern European grandparents; there should be some race memory, shouldn't there, an uncanny familiar flavour? What did it taste of, this romantic bark?

Nothing. It tasted of nothing at all.

TRISTESSE OF GERMINATION

It is time for a confession.

The best bit about growing from seed, other than cheapness and variety, is the thrill of germination. Isn't it? After all the palaver, the different compost types, the tamping and watering, what could be more exciting than seeing the shoots emerge? Bravely they push aside immense coir-fibre boulders; heads bent or with their frail white root exposed, they struggle to overcome the obstacles which you, their careless sower, have strewn in their path. Their troubles are moving: the unfortunate cap of seed coat stuck to a courgette seedling, like an infant that has tried to dress itself; a single zinnia, lone survivor of its people, simultaneously green and pink as an over-sucked penny sweet. Alas, it is no beauty, but it has a lovely personality.

Then something disturbing happens. Once the seeds have germinated and begun to grow, I lose momentum. They need pricking out and potting on but, like a bad parent, my interest has turned to their younger, more vulnerable successors. Rather than attend to their teenaged needs, I keep on sowing. We ought to try those orange nasturtiums, I decide. I want, no, I need, cinnamon basil and a more magenta honesty; is there anywhere open this late at night? I know I've only just thought of it, but now I can't wait, not another minute. This is an emergency.

Yet there is worse: far worse. It pains me even to type this; despite such interest and passion, so many books read, I am not always quite as careful with the new seedlings as I might be. As I have mentioned, I am by nature clumsy and graceless, small-handed, stubby of finger; that isn't all. There is a recklessness, even a slapdash attitude. I behave as if the fragile stems and tender leaves of my laboriously hatched plantlets, insufficiently thinned, hurriedly and roughly squished into already heavily full containers, have ceased to interest me.

The reasons are not pretty. First, there is time. In a garden there is always slightly more to do than one can manage; that is the point. And, given the infinite needs of one's existing plants, the bare minimum of picking-tying-pruning-weeding-clearing-feeding-watering, let alone chitting and mulching and fleecing and forcing and netting and staking and dressing and aerating and hardening and bud-rubbing, who then has half-hours to spare for batches of flimsy new plants, in need of several participles of their own: thinning, pinching, pricking, transplanting? Shouldn't they be able to totter off and fend for themselves, like ducklings?

The second, once again, is space. This is the great difference between gardeners with swathes of border and those bravely persisting with only, or mostly, containers. We, the latter, have no elbow room. With immense Great Dixter-style borders there is always a place for another few *Penstemon* 'Sour Grapes' or delphiniums (always in an odd number), whereas with a container, once its owner has reached a certain level of gardening mania, there is no scope. In my flowerpots and window boxes and trugs and buckets, a Darwinian struggle for resources is taking place. It is more like a school playground than a civilised pleasure garden: the crab apple, depressed since it was given away in a cardboard tube at a summer fair, as anyone might be, vies with the small but tough oregano to rob the self-seeded aquilegia of nutrients, while the remaining surface is slowly colonised by wild strawberry plants, coaxed since they were runners to put down their own roots and now just about old enough to grow alone, crowding out my sweet deep-orange violas, a couple of plucky rockets (both white-flowered salad and yellow-flowered wild) and a single lavender 'Hidcote', secretly drawing up plans to climb down out of this pot and find some decent soil.

I feel like a Victorian father of many plain daughters – oh Lord, here's another one to find a husband for. The uncomfortable truth is this: however tenderly we nurse our babies through germination and sprouting and that awkward seed-leaf stage, once they are old enough to be transplanted we begin to hate them, just a little. Where are we to put them? Ignoring the fact that the poor bay still hasn't had its topsoil renewed, could I make room for these parsley seedlings behind it, among the wild garlic? If I turn the pot, a whole couple of centimetres are revealed, once I move this mildewed sage . . . except the soil is solid with desperate questing roots, and won't the Moroccan mint suffocate it, and isn't that a snowdrop bulb and where can I put this sentimentally important mug handle?

Wait . . . am I at last the proud parent of a tiny self-seeded parsley baby? I try a leaf; it reveals its true identity: leaf celery, a metallic cuckoo in the nest. Sadly the summer savory, grown to eat with beans as instructed by Pat, hasn't made it. On the other hand, every seed in my recklessly huge pinches of that rather bristly kale has germinated and, after foisting half of them off on alarmed acquaintances, I am unable to throw the extras out but bitterly resent them. I seem to spend the evenings walking around and around the garden like a soul in Purgatory, looking for another pot into which to force the survivors.

Third, there is the Bible. The Bible, as one might expect, is big on growing. Like many young heathens, my primary education was vigorously Anglican, filled with parables and the Lord's Prayer and, once a year, a musical based on a the Old Testament. Certain tales sank deeply into my suggestible mind, proving particularly hard to shake: the Parable of the Sower, for example.

Like all lazy gardeners I love the idea of broadcast sowing. One minute we are chucking handfuls of seed gracefully on well-tilled soil; the next: behold! A meadow! But let us examine the parable for sources of anxiety. Presumably the sower in question was an experienced agrarian professional, the soil much-cultivated sandy silt washed down by the River Jordan. Then given that of four seeds sown, one fell on rocks, one lay on a path and was trodden on, one was choked by thorns or was eaten by a camel or otherwise foundered *and only one flourished*, what chance do mine have, at the hands of an ignorant novelist? I don't know about Galilee but in England we have squirrels, and really quite ferocious robins; larger seeds are ill-omened from the first and what of the tiny ones, trapped under a particularly heavy piece of grit? Oh my darlings: what will become of you?

I have one final theory about the tristesse of germination: the pleasure is in the anticipation, like parties, or hot baths. As the Edwardian Scotsman-turned-Canadian-cowboy Robert Service put it, in his 'The Spell of the Yukon':

> Yet it isn't the gold that I'm wanting
> So much as just finding the gold …
> It's the stillness that fills me with peace.

Sowing is gardening in miniature: soil under your nails, solitude and minute focus, the thrill of potential and the triumph of hope over experience, yet again. When we sow, we're not really aiming for the gaudy results the seed packets promise. We merely want the feeling it gives us: to keep sowing, and never worry about the consequences. Service was right; it is peace.

LATE SPRING

'Gardening became a secret vice for me, a vice because I always felt guilty when I indulged in it, knowing there were many other things I ought to be doing.'

Elizabeth Jane Howard, *Slipstream*

THE GREATEST SMELL
ON EARTH

Hares are boxing, lambs are bleating, foals are staggering about on paperclip legs as if fresh from office parties and, in gardens all over the land, there are sounds of snorting, as apparently sane women and men fill their lungs with balmy air.

Because isn't this the clearest proof of spring? We may be able to see greenery at last, discard jumpers and eschew stew but it is that first vernal sniff, the soft sappy filaments of sap or pollen hitting our olfactory nerves, which tell us it is time to begin. We know that the earth is magical; it's just that we need reminding.

Gardening magazines are obsessed with scent but they mean flowers. Make a garden which will satisfy all your senses, they implore, lest we forget smell entirely and cover every leaf in brown paper; no, paint it with creosote . . . no, none of these, because, to some of us, each of these smells glorious too.

I would, if I could, buy perennials which reeked of fresh tarmac. Those richly bubbling cauldrons on the backs of vans, the matte black bricks waiting to be melted; it is far from the sweet breath of narcissi but my father and I both take deep greedy breaths of it whenever we pass. I have been known to press my nose to freshly weatherproofed fences. And let's not even start on old books, or babies' heads, or Guerlain's Mitsouko; now, if David Austin could sort out a rose which smelled of those, I'd be more interested.

For the indecisive, choosing plants for the garden stretches us to our limits. Everything is so dangerously tempting already, before we have factored in hardiness, culinary value, difficulty of obtaining and attractiveness to ladybirds; scent just pushes us over the edge. Besides, so many edible plants smell fantastic without even trying. During a purgatorial Greek holiday, where the beach was grey grit and oiled Ukrainians basked like walruses on the only sun-loungers while the few white Englishers crouched by rocks, we lived for our evening visit to a little bakery. It offered not only air-conditioning and barely sweetened aniseed rusks but also a basil plant, whose smell was so entrancing, sweet and deep as clove flowers, that I invented reasons to visit, like a teenager mid-crush. By an amazing coinci-

I led us, totally by accident, to the island's sole florist where, among dusty Christmas cacti and memorial plaques, only the most inventive threats stopped me from stowing several small cinnamon-basil plants about my person.

Yet even this little garden is full of scent. I don't mean flowers but the leaves, which I walk around inhaling like a confused smoker: the sweet armpit warmth of fig leaves, the mouthwatering fizz of lemon verbena, the bracing resin of rosemary. Their evanescence is slightly dementing, particularly for the greedy cook-gardener. This year, I promise myself, I'll not only add sweet cicely leaves to rhubarb, and 'Attar of Roses' pelargonium to blackberries, but make blackcurrant-leaf tea and put baby vine leaves in salad and even investigate the fig-leaf ice cream of which I have heard tantalising rumours.

After a lifetime of writing, smells are still so difficult to capture. Christopher Lloyd divided them into 'moral' and 'immoral' and this shorthand for freshness versus sexiness goes some way. Might similes be better: mothballs, pepper, cat's pee, marmalade, fathers, puppies, gloves? William Sole in his 1798 *Menthae Britannicae*, which I came to via Richard Mabey's *Flora Britannica* (a book itself so spellbindingly diverting that opening its index is like entering a dangerous maze), described water mint, *M. aquatica*, as having a smell 'exactly like that of a ropy chimney in a wet summer, where wood fires have been kept in winter-time'. I have the very chimney; soon I will sniff water mint, and report.

And, as all thinking persons know, there is nothing like petrichor. Petrichor is the compound released when rain falls on soil, named (romantically) after the Greek words for stone and the lifeblood of the gods and derived (less romantically) from chemicals secreted by plants during dry weather to inhibit growth. It makes one close one's eyes and inhale elemental breaths: water, decay, rust, life.

When dressing, I alternate between three different perfumes, two of which are combinations of incense and spice and the other which really does evoke fig-leaves, but what I would give to smell of petrich—

Actually, I think I may already do.

WHAT TO GROW WHEN YOU CAN'T GROW LEMONS

L emon balm is almost the perfect plant: fragrant, edible, adaptable, easy to grow. Unfortunately, it is also revolting

Why does no one admit this? It's in every list of desirable plants, yet there is something unspeakable in its scent: a syrupy sweetness beside the tang, artificial as furniture polish or car sweets. Its taste is worse: like a squirt of bathroom-freshener. One is told to appreciate its easy-going, tisane-enriching, bee-encouraging ways. No: it is vile. Treat it as a weed and rip it out.

Lemon thyme: every year you disappoint me. Why do we keep pretending you'll stick around? You make these promises and I keep trying to please you: more grit, less water, less fuss. It isn't fuss; it's love. But, every winter, you leave me. When will I learn?

Lemon grass is easy; you simply shove two unpromising supermarket stalks into a jar of water and wait for roots. It's magical: the twenty-first-century sophisticate's equivalent of cress on kitchen towel, with an exciting citrus knife-blade edge. However, all that you produce is a couple of leafy stems which, once you have planted them out, will be less useful than the original stalk and much more worrying: they won't survive the winter. Don't even try.

Which leaves us with lemon verbena: a reputedly tricky plant. I have been lucky with mine, perhaps because I fleece it thoroughly in winter and for the rest of the year treat it meanly, never transplanting it to a larger pot or removing its dead, delicious-smelling leaves. If you succeed, it is everything you might wish for, provided that, every spring, you remind yourself not to panic. It isn't dead. Long after everything else has burst into leaf, your lemon verbena will prevaricate, its spindly twigs mocking you for not having invested in a cloche, a straw jacket, perhaps a three-quarter-length mink, to keep it warm. Do not despair; don't throw it out. Just wait, and wait; at last the leaves will come.

Then, like a tired couple away on a long weekend, you will remember what you first saw in each other. Mine lives by the back door, where its dry spear-shaped leaves in a flat mid-green do nothing for the view but everything for our elbows and legs when we brush past it on our way outside. The scent is fabulous: a resinous sherbety zest, exactly as one might hope a lemon tree's bark might taste. Its most obvious glory is as tea. When fresh, it turns the water an interestingly urinous yellow and tastes delicious; when dry, it is less amusing but almost as good. Culinarily, try it whenever you might include lemon zest or thyme, which covers almost everything: pushed messily into the cavity of fish; poked in the crevices of a joint of pork; chopped finely for a herby omelette or a holiday-evoking tangle of mint and feta and bitter leaves; pressed on the bottom of a cake tin (plain madeira, peach and almond, raspberry); best of all, its smaller leaves torn and included in a salad.

Why stop there? I should make lemon verbena granita, maybe even a panna cotta. I'll do it one day, sooner rather than later, when the children are grown up and my lovely leafy plant and I have the house to ourselves.

FOR THE LOVE OF LEGUMES

I can hardly keep up with the garden. Even apart from the usual participles, there are so many new seedlings to pot on, both favourites and bold experiments: *Cerinthe major* 'Purpurascens', with its sharky blue-grey bloom; *Ammi majus*, bishop's weed, for hoverflies; agretti so I can pretend to be by the sea eating samphire, and puntarelle, so I can pretend to be Italian; *cime di rapa*, juicy bunches of turnip greens which, when sautéed with garlic, are so bitter yet sweet that other vegetables seem wilfully one-dimensional; cucamelons, gearing up for their annual failure; gherkins, to compensate for the cucamelons; leeks, because it's always good to fail at something new; the beautifully bronze sunflower 'Earth Walker', despite its irritating name; the Californian poppies whose orange flowers transfixed me at Waterperry; yet more basil and parsley and chervil; and at least eight, no, nine, whoops, a dozen varieties of bean and pea.

Like an adulterer who claims, every time, that they can't help falling in love, legumes are just one of my manifold obsessions. How could they not be? Look at this single borlotti bean, creamily skinned, flashed and flecked with wine like the work of a deranged Renaissance artist; consider lilac-flowered black-seeded 'Cobra', or 'Orca', like baby killer whales, or 'Annelino Verde', its pod curled like a speckled prawn. Choice is impossible; one can only succumb. It is by refusing to grow dwarf beans that I can limit myself. Get thee behind me, 'Pawnee', navy bean and 'Shirokostruczkovnia'; I need the maximum number of beans from the tiniest possible soil. This is the battery farm of gardens, and yield is king.

Beans are brilliant. They are pretty, productive, nutritious and scientifically interesting, although I am distressed by the continuing uncertainty about tendril twining-direction, and whether or not it's the same as bathwater in plug holes. Their leaves have strange adhesive qualities. They even carry a whiff of danger; eating them raw exposes us to low levels of phyto-haemagglutinin, which is what we boil away when we cook them dried. I eat most of my crop off the vine; if the body accumulates phytohaemagglutinin, an interesting but rather short future awaits. But then apple seeds contain cyanide and, whether they're killing me or making me stronger, I love them so much I save them until last, as little treats.

Last year my favourite legumes struggled: the lilac-flowered 'Cosse Violette' and the buttery flattish 'Cornetti Meraviglia de Venise', the runner 'Scarlet Emperor', mainly for its flowers, the Asian yardlong, a handful of anonymous peas roaming wild at the bottom of the biscuit tin and the anomalies: Borlotto Sanguino 'Bloody'; 'Cherokee Trail of Tears', because of its history; 'Lazy Housewife', out of clear, if nonspecific, feminist duty. The problem was toilet rolls, and my supermarket's decision to shrink their inner-tube size, without respecting the needs of the French-bean-growing community who hitherto relied on rolls of a decent width as the ideal growing vessel. Tantalisingly, not all manufacturers have followed. I eye my friends' lavatories hungrily; any office toilet is at risk.

Yes, I could reduce uncertainty, could know the joy of a bean glut at long last, simply by growing several plants each of a couple of common varieties. I could also refuse to become a woman who leaves important meetings with stolen toilet-roll tubes bulging in her coat pockets. But where would be the fun in that?

THE GARDEN AT NIGHT

There is not enough time; nowhere near. I go out in my pyjamas to check on the new *Trachelospermum jasminoides*; sow sorrel and turn seed trays between paragraphs; find myself, when I am meant to be concentrating on a difficult plot point, outside on all fours, grubbing up the first signs of the creeping buttercup, my old foe. And, after dinner, by the feeble light through the kitchen door, I drift outside with the tools of my trade: unwashed plastic pots containing unpleasant surprises, a sack of home-made potting compost, based on a secret recipe: Ikea coir briquette + contents of last month's microgreens experiment + couple of worm casts from under a brick + rain-saturated sand.

Darkness is never the right environment for sowing seeds. But often, as many working parents know, it is only when too tired to write and the kids are pretending to sleep that there is time to garden and, unless we do it now, chaos will engulf us. This takes us into dangerous territory: the world of hands-free lighting. Unless one has a genuinely tool-heavy career, attending drainage emergencies, perhaps, or catching nocturnal mammals, there is never any excuse for serious torch-wear. I have often dreamed of floodlights, or a small helper holding out their wind-up ladybird light like a tame Prometheus, and have almost come to terms with the fact that it may never happen. But my own expedient, a long series of rechargeables and lanterns and LEDs and flashlights, never ceases to disappoint.

Perhaps all addicts have, beyond the depths they vowed never to plumb, the barrels they tried not to scrape and ended up scraping, a final sacred line they will not cross. For me, it is the head torch. We ardent gardeners abandoned common decency some time ago: too much mud in our lives, too many murdered slug babies and adjustable knee-pads and secret trips to skips. But some vestigial instinct for self-preservation reminds me that, although a head torch makes sense – hands-free, difficult to drop – it would be fatal. The border between eccentric and frothingly insane must not be breached; besides, I can't face the laughter. I must resist it. Every day without an adjustable Velcro headband is another little triumph.

FLOW

Sometimes, in cartoons, an anvil falls from the sky. Sometimes, on suburban streets, sinkholes appear and swallow bicycles and little dogs in an instant.

2008 was the year of the sinkhole. A lifetime of imagining the worst offered no insurance whatsoever against things going wrong and still more wrong and, in the depths of the dark wood, what saved me was not God, or denial, or increasingly even hope, but my tiny garden. I would come home from work, totter through the house and straight out of the kitchen door, where the cool green garden waited to distract me with nibblings, wiltings, etiolation and a thousand other tiny misfortunes. I didn't wonder then why its spell was so strong, how it could calm so entirely when nothing else had any power but now I do. The answer is flow.

Flow is the secret of life, or at least of contentment. Mihaly Csikszentmihalyi, the magnificently named psychologist who identified it, describes it as total absorption in an activity for its own sake, so that hours and pain and tiredness and worry vanish, enabling us to live purely – and contentedly – in the moment. It is what drives us to assemble jigsaws, or sing, or collect *Star Wars* figurines; the reason for climbing; the point of needlepoint; the only conceivable explanation for golf. Flow occurs when we are utterly focused on the small tasks and pleasures before us – will this work? How do I fix that? – rather than on our own troubles, or global crises, or the black dogs that snap at our ankles the moment we open a newspaper. And gardening, with its combination of sensual engagement, constant minor puzzles and the illusion of progress, is, for my money, the best of the lot; dirtier than Sudoku, more tiring than knitting but, by God, it works. I am never calmer than when inspecting the plague of tiny snails on my spring greens, pausing to nibble a leaf myself, spotting a yellow one, admiring the tracery of veins on its underside, the sunlight playing through the darker upper surface. Look, hard, at the inside of an apple: the star-shaped core, pips like tiny chestnut tears. Lose yourself in wood grain; think about the miraculous effort required by every xylem and phloem, the genius of each nascent cell, to make something so lovely, without regard for you.

Better yet, the effect is portable. As I was once told, when unfortunately far too young and miserable to pay attention, the best way to turn off neurotic spiralling thoughts is to observe, wherever you are. For me, it works best in nature. Just as three-year-olds can, sometimes, be distracted from hysteria by a funny bus, most fretting or sadness can momentarily be soothed by a municipal rose petal, deepening from shell-pink to blush to plum; the beading of dew on an *Alchemilla mollis*'s parasol leaf; the skilful pruning of wisteria on park railings. It's like taking a rest on the landing of a long flight of stairs; the brain has a chance to gather itself.

This was discovered long before mindfulness colouring books were invented. Voltaire was a great gardener, even if he mostly did the shopping ('artichoke bulbs and as much as possible of lavender, thyme, rosemary, mint, basil, rue strawberry bushes, pinks, thadicée, balm, tarragon, sariette, burnet, sage and hyssop to cleanse our sins, etc. etc. etc.') and others did the actual labour. His *Candide* is an unexpectedly cheering book, steering its hero open-eyed through true suffering (the Lisbon earthquake, torture, slavery) and leading the reader to conclude that cultivating their garden is the only sane response. Ninety-five years later, in a superficially wilder garden, Henry David Thoreau agreed: 'Am I not partly leaves and vegetable mould myself?'

Even without being chin-bearded transcendentalists, we can admit he was on to something. For Thoreau, losing himself in the savagery, the beauty and, best of all, the intricacy of nature offered peace. He is worshipped in North America but few readers elsewhere will have dared face *Walden*; at least for its nature writing, more of us should. It is deliciously obsessive: a compulsive ode to 'the tonic of wilderness'. Chapter Seventeen, in which spring arrives, is extraordinary: the honeycomb patterns and crackles of thawing ice; the shades of sand and clay; the shapes formed by the rivulets, like 'the laciniated, lobed, and imbricated thalluses of some lichens; or you are reminded of coral, of leopard's paws or birds' feet, of brains or lungs or bowels, and vegetable leaves'. We don't know if Thoreau was escaping from anxiety, sexual confusion or merely his family's pencil factory but, by immersing himself in detail, noting the cost of 'white line for crow fence' ($0.02) or wondering what it might be like to eat a woodchuck raw, he freed himself, at least for a time.

Nature is a such a physical pleasure that it is tempting to sink into it entirely. Who can see the first egg-yolk-yellow crocus on a grassy verge and not want to push their face inside? Or to put a newly hatched conker in their mouth or kneel down in fresh young spring grass and champ it like a foal? Please don't say it's just me.

Don't tell me that other people, during the many long lonely intervals of childhood, didn't fall in love with the blistered sun-warmed paint on a door, or the beauty of old lichened bricks, or susurrating grasses? I'm sure it made me a gardener, this self-soothing alertness, this urgent need to look. Maybe it makes writers, too. Monet wrote: *Je dois peut-être aux fleurs d'avoir été peintre* – 'I perhaps owe having become a painter to flowers.' Writers are often asked what made them write; I can't answer that for myself, let alone interpret Monet, but I think he might have meant that the intense feelings evoked by colour and form made him need to express himself, and he chose paint; but he also became a great gardener.

If you are even remotely plant-obsessed, I suspect you understand. Scent and colour, fragility, nature itself are hard to describe, but to garden with them is to bring them closer. The impulse is the same. We live in a world of ceaseless human misery, nude selfies, celebrity dunderheads and online venom. The pain of it is almost too much to bear but you will bear it, you almost certainly will, if you go out into a garden.

SHISO

To initiates, its name alone is magical. Victorian gardeners – and still some modern plant catalogues – knew it as *Perilla frutescens* and used it as a bedding plant, thanks to its heart-shaped leaves in apple-green, or with magenta undersides or entirely purple.

Oh, Mrs Beeton: what a pleasure you missed. Like eighteenth-century European jugginses believing that tomatoes were poisonous and ignoring potatoes until Marie Antoinette wore potato blossom in her hair, think how much happier the widowed Queen Victoria would have been if an under-gardener had persuaded her to taste those pretty leaves: aromatic as basil but fresher, touched with tarragon and mint. And meanwhile, in Japan, they had named it shiso and this secret plant came alive.

I met it first in a plastic-bamboo-lined Japanese restaurant as a small skewered pinwheel of pork and herbs, charcoal-grilled by an unsmiling squid tentacle-master. You may see it garnishing sushi, looking like a lime-leaf with serrated wavy nettle-edges – eat it. You may spot it in an Asian supermarket on a tiny Styrofoam tray, at a pound a leaf – buy it. Forget banana mint and Vietnamese coriander; this is a herb you must try.

Or perhaps don't. Because one leaf, two leaves, will not be enough; you will not rest before you have tasted it again, introduced it to your friends. But who can afford a daily supply of charcoal-grilled pork pinwheels? You will think: Aha, I'll grow it. And then you are doomed.

Try to find a young shiso plant. Keep trying. Years ago, lost in the Versailles of garden centres, largely devoted to gas-fired barbecues and poor sad bougainvilleas in antiqued 50-kilogram urns, I spotted one, huddled alone among the standard olives. Only £7? Here, take my purse. Have the shirt off my back. I nursed it, stroked it, loved it until it died and now, like a forlorn suitor, cannot leave any display of bedding or herbs until I have scoured it for my lost love, shiso, never to be found again.

Shiso seed is not difficult to buy. Almost every supplier sells it, although from their descriptions they clearly have no idea of its riches. The problem is freshness. I have sown and sown and only succeeded once, with a packet from Otter Farm; I can almost smell its fragrance on my hands. It was like growing gold. For weeks, every salad contained three or four leaves, torn as gently as if I were distributing communion wafers. My tiny plant grew until, by early autumn, it resembled a bushy little Christmas tree, with discreet starry flowers. Ridiculous: I could have feasted on it all summer but the harvest had seemed too precious, or I was too scared and now I had more leaves than I could use.

The answer was pork; it often is. The butcher suggested a chunk of rolled shoulder, cutting a pocket for this herb I kept trying to describe to him. He was clearly unhappy.

'Why not try rosemary?' he asked, as if I planned to stuff it with grass clip-pings. 'It goes well with pork. Trust me.'

I knew I was right, that the stuffed pork shoulder was a masterstroke, yet still I could not pick the leaves. The pork went into the freezer. No occasion seemed to deserve it; no guest or family member would understand the majesty, the sacrifice. Eventually I cooked the pork with cider and juniper berries. Autumn ripened; the nights grew cold and my shiso began to shed its leaves like a blanket over all the tiny mustards and lettuces I had sown too late to thrive. Its flowers promised seeds, which means self-seeding; hungrily I waited, and no seed appeared. The leaves were about to become unusable. At last, in panic, I turned to thoughts of preservation.

I have hundreds of cookery books; the question, I was confident, would be which ingenious recipe to try. Disaster: none of them had even thought of shiso. So I turned to my fellow obsessive, Joy Larkcom. In her embarrassingly pleasurable *Oriental Vegetables* she mentions vinegar made of shiso and umeboshi-plum pickling brine; I toyed with entering a black market of unobtainable fruit and school-laboratory steel tubing before turning sadly to the internet, where I discovered a Japanese packed-lunch blog. On the top shelf of the fridge, among the rejected jams, there now sits a ramekin half-filled with washed and dried shiso leaves, individually salted, whose outcome remains unclear: does it become a relish? Will all that shiso, all that love, amount to nothing more than a slimy teaspoon of vaguely exotic disappointment?

A week has passed. Under its blanket of clingfilm, my entire shiso harvest awaits me, and I am too terrified to peek.

THE PERFECT OUTFIT

One of the greatest joys of gardening is the chance to wear fabulous clothes. These fall into two categories. Unfortunately, I am in the wrong one.

The first is Gardening Glamour, whose handbook is Ursula Buchan's *Garden People*. Masquerading as a collection of the photographs of the late plantswoman Valerie Finnis, it is actually an evil recruitment manual. Merely open it: gardening without kilts and Hitchcockian silk and ancestral tweed will seem a waste of life. Could I get away with a Dame Miriam Rothschild-style turban, or Nancy Lancaster's sexy yellow scarf, or the high-waisted corduroy and rakish gaucho hat of Rhoda, Lady Birley, as she firmly grips those scarlet parrot-bill loppers? Vita Sackville-West's startling leather gaiters do look practical, almost stirring, particularly if one bears in mind Noel Coward's description of her as 'Lady Chatterley above the waist and the gamekeeper below'. By the basic error of not having been yet born, I wasted the best years of my life, when I could have been fan-training peach trees and forcing strawberries at Waterperry Horticultural School for Women, in hard-wearing yet flattering dungarees, stout shoes and a Daphne du Maurier haircut.

So what are the alternatives? Glamour has left gardening behind; other than Monty Don's marvellous trousers-and-braces, celebrity gardeners seem contractually obliged to wear the least exciting clothing possible: unelitist, wash-and-wear. Where is the joy in that? The solution, I believe, is to embrace the extreme: by combining one's favourite garments in outfits so mad and terrible that one loves them, despite themselves.

My father, who otherwise dresses as a mature professional, rakes leaves in flared cords with lichens growing in the crevices, Green Flash tennis shoes and an Eighties baby-blue C&A anorak, which sheds luminous puffs of stuffing over the lawn. I have inherited his unerring sartorial eye. Little is more satisfying than to dress properly in one's most ancient and peculiar clothes, welcoming compost and cobweb and worm urine as sacred unguents. If we ignore the many times when, late at night, a little post-party in one's fantastic new shoes, one is suddenly moved to prune the extremely thorny blackberry, don't most of us secretly love the unhinged drama of our gardening clothes? Mine include my favourite T-shirt, bought in my teens, now faded to mole-grey and mysteriously small; a turquoise rollneck Irish jumper almost wholly unravelled below the elbow; suede-soft jeans so dated that even the most desperate charity shop would 'rag' them, which is as low as clothes can go. Yes, I love my MAC lipsticks, my fabulous gold brogues and newest pencil skirt, but this is my outfit of greatest joy. I probably wear it a little more than I should. The Kurdish corner-shop men no longer comment when, lightly thorn-scratched, my entire front surface coated in leaves and compost gleanings like a demented badge of pride, I drop in for emergency teabags. If I have been soaked through by a leaping hosepipe, they kindly avert their eyes.

Then there is mud. Perhaps, deep in our amygdala, human beings crave silt and swamp and muddiness: a literal *nostalgie de boue*. So, much as I would like to become a clean-fingernailed woman in a cashmere cape and Swiss gardening culottes, the truth is that I am never happier than when absolutely filthy, dressed like a mudlark and, best of all, my feet warm and dry in my beloved olive-green galoshes.

I wish every gardener could have galoshes as fine as mine. They were a birthday present; the strange but unerring choice of Em, my oldest friend. These galoshes are not pretty. Owners of beach-hut-themed potting sheds and replica shepherd's cabins would baulk. Yet, in their extreme waterproofing and rubbery lack of pretension, they are perfect: almost as good as bare feet. They have given me more pleasure than any trowel or ball of twine; you are, they seem to say, a gardener. Go forth and get filthy. And, oh, I do.

PESTILENCE

Deer are shy and beautiful. Squirrels do amusing things with acorns. Pigeons are delicious, and wildlife-starved town children can try to keep woodlice in matchboxes filled with leaves. None of this can be said for vine weevils: the low-lives of the garden pest world.

Vine weevils make woolly aphids seem attractive, earwigs potentially loving pets. The pea-sized adults, a matte dirty black, will nibble at anything precious, especially in a container. However, these waving-antlered horrors are beauties compared to their maggoty larvae, soft and white as death, hiding in the soil while they binge secretly on plant roots: far more destructive and curiously disgusting, as if one has been nursing a parasite. In panic, one sends off thousands of pounds and receives a tiny tray of sticky fluff, allegedly teeming with the vine-weevil nemesis, nematode *Steinernema kraussei*. It is stored in the fridge, which involves lying to one's family; it's an uncomfortable business, planning mail-order genocide. And when at last one finds time to apply one's biological weapon, mixing it with a broom handle in a watering can, then worrying about the insufficiently detailed instructions (should one drench or splash?), despite the leap of faith one has taken there is no end to their pillaging.

This is the answer: a night mission.

There are few more satisfying activities than a little light murder. All pests are a joy to kill; the iridescent charms of rosemary beetle, slow-moving millipedes, a variety of caterpillars. After a difficult day I relax by searching for leaf-miners: pellets of malice digging mazy scar tunnels in spinach and chicory. But vine weevil-hunting by torchlight is the connoisseur's choice. Like a leopard stalking tender baby gnus, I take my prey very seriously, inspecting each pot and, in some cases, each leaf, front and back, for the adults, while issuing muttered threats. And, oh, the satisfaction when, after a lengthy stake-out, I spot one of the little devils crouching on the poor redcurrant and, before it can play dead, I can perform my patented scoop-and-grab in order to crush it into the fluorescent goo it so richly deserves to become.

Does that stop them? Not remotely. If, like a giant, one put an ear to the soil and heard its secrets, every pot would be crackling with the sound of larvae hatching. For sanity's sake, one must ignore this, dreading the discovery of further evidence: a glistening, sickly-pale gobbety crescent moon. Were one to pick out every last one, the next plant along would be just as badly infested by the grubs' acrobatic mothers. Nothing is enough. And we town-dwellers are left with a dilemma: everything I have ever read instructs us to dispose of the contaminated compost. Where? Soil is specifically forbidden in council recycling bags; the pavement outside is crowded with Peugeots and scooters, not convenient flower-beds. So, in the spirit of damned compromise on which most of my garden efforts are based, I sneak the odd clump into the household rubbish, with broken crocks and snail shells, and distribute the rest, laboriously but imperfectly picked over, in the cat-scarred chaos beneath the sarcococca, from which it is but a short stroll for all the freshly hatched virgin soldiers to my waiting strawberry plants.

EARLY SUMMER

'If it looks like a clover, the operation is over;
If it looks like a dahlia, the operation's a failure.'

Colorectal surgeons' proverb for
haemorrhoidectomies

AN UNERRING EYE

As canaries were once used in mines, and the first pancake is always a write-off, I would like to offer myself as a sacrifice for the common good, as a false-economy equipment selector.

Unlike most reviewers, I am not compromised by sponsorship or personal foible. All I am interested in is finding the best and most reliable item of technology and labour-saving devices. As objectively as any human can, possibly more so, I research every possible pro, each con, cross-referencing consumer tests, writing shortlists far into the night. Then, unswervingly as a laser, I make my choice: always, and uncompromisingly, the worst one possible.

Shouldn't this strange talent be harnessed? We could hire me out as a sort of anti-consumer: Incapability Mendelson. My record of making poor yet heavily researched choices is almost unbroken: the slow laptops, the saggy yoga ball, the bathroom taps (twice), miniature freezer, Christmas trees, simultaneously scentless and needle-dropping, the blender, Barry the Shed, every toaster. I'm even better when it comes to gardenware. Let us take, as an example, my long-handled loppers; except that we can't, because they are almost too heavy to lift.

Loppers are a marvellous invention: sharp-jawed, with extendable handles and therefore perfect for long-distance snipping. I had been flummoxed by the ivy blossom and rose petals tumbling in orgiastic plenty on my mustard greens: long-handled secateurs seemed a marvellous solution. By chance, this was a rare month in which no gardening magazine was running a lopper test; I could have searched through the glossy pile of collapsing back issues which teeters, like a Damoclean accordion, above my desk but, surely, even I could choose a reasonable pair.

Should I go to a garden centre, try a few, and pick. Compulsions do not work that way. The mind cannot be defeated. Just as with little-known works of crime fiction, or Turkish orange aubergine-seed, or fruit dehydrators, discovering that such things exist makes me need to possess them. So, online, I made my choice: a healthy compromise, it seemed, between weight and reach and price. The box in which they arrived could have housed a teenage crocodile. They were long and, with much twisting, could be made a few centimetres longer; they were built to last, of sturdy steel and were, therefore, ideally suited for a muscular park-keeper, in a thicket, being attacked by bears. For years, I carried on bravely, balancing tiptoe on bricks and chairs to snip the highest ivy stems I could reach, which renewed themselves, almost before my eyes, as they dropped snails and indestructible leaves on the soil beneath. Meanwhile, the taller stems grew above me, tangling with the creamy roses to form a waving thicket several metres high, blocking the sunlight, shedding their flowers.

At last I cracked. It was time, I conceded, to invest in telescopic shears This time, however, I would investigate every option, not stint on price but buy them from a proper stockist and, armed with the correct tool, by evening I would have cleared the trellis. And so, cautiously, affordably, I made my investment. The shears, impressively long-handled and pleasingly lightweight, had metres of black cord and even an extra blade: an excellent choice, virtually professional. I hauled the thing out of the back door and set to work.

Yet nothing is light enough not to grow heavy, and still heavier, when 2 metres long and held at an angle from one's body. Dauntless, I changed position, pulling with ever-growing confidence on the cord that sliced so efficiently through the stems and it was only when I was utterly exhausted, which could not be said for the ivy, that I stopped. Feebly, but very carefully, I gathered the leaves and stems and clots of dusty cobweb into green recyclable waste bags, lest in the fecund depths of my compost bin the shoots regenerated. I hoicked the shears' handle-ends on to my thigh to close them, as in photographs, began to wrap the cord safely around the handles, carried it with very few incidents to the corner in which I planned to stable it (well, yes, of course it would rust, but who has a shed large enough for one of these?) and, only then, noticed something odd about the cord.

Slowly, noisily, I lowered it again, avoiding pots and limbs until the head was within eyeshot, much like Hemingway's Old Man reeling in his fish. Then I saw the truth: on this, its maiden voyage, the black string was almost cut through.

I am back to wobbly chairs and the heavy loppers; I deserve no better. There have been many other triumphs: the netting I spent an entire Saturday attaching to the wall for my barely weaned 'Sugar Ann' and 'Purple Podded' peas, only to discover, on Sunday, the net trampled to the ground by cats abseiling off the trellis and the seedlings ravished by the slugs which had waited until I went in for the night. There is the wall-mounted hose reel no wall can stand, which now lies in the bay pot, ready to take on anyone stupid enough to hope for access; the cheap ratchet secateurs and the cheaper heavy-duty secateurs and the wooden-handled secateurs, simultaneously blunt and rusty; the small parasol; the compost riddler, its mesh so fine and my compost so rough that, after sieving perhaps a tablespoonful, I gave up and hid it from myself behind a Bag for Life stuffed with plastic pots.

Kipling wrote of the under-gardeners in great British country houses, grubbing about on paths with broken knives. That sounds perfectly reasonable to me. Herb snippers and pot brushes and Dutch bulb planters are the scented candles of gardening: the gifts one goes on giving, rather than keeping for oneself. It is only with an old spoon, strong kitchen scissors, a child's rusty trowel, a lidless felt-tip, too much string and one's own stubby muddy hands that one can work miracles.

I have left until last my greatest disappointment. I can hardly bear to type it: my cold frame shame. The first example, cheap, online, was an inevitable disaster, surprising only to me. Its replacement was double the price, from a proper firm. How bad could it be?

Bad.

Embarrassingly, I had also paid Jarek, the local Polish odd-job man cum-parachute-instructor, to assemble it. In the meantime, I had rather brilliantly rescued a sash window from a skip. A solution dawned: why not accept my impracticality and ask him to build me a proper one? It couldn't be more expensive than buying yet another mail-order mistake. Jarek is a lovely intelligent man but the gap between his English and my Builder was wider than either of us had realised. The result was a wide, deep crate made of plywood, a material which ripples and warps at the mere thought of rain, barely insulated with heavy rotten lids of fragile glass. It is the Petit Trianon of garden structures; the only object I have ever designed and, demonstrably, the world's worst cold frame. Is that not something of which to be proud?

FEEDING THE SOIL,
NOT THE PLANT

This is, like so many helpful mottoes, maddeningly imprecise. Plants are *in* soil; one can hardly stop them from taking a slurp of compost, like a schoolchild scoffing its packed lunch on the bus. Anyway, what does 'feed' mean? Like a baby, with a teaspoon? Playing Helicopters? And, if we are avoiding fertilisers, the turquoise granules of yesteryear, aren't hoof-and-horn and comfrey liquid and bone meal all fertilisers too?

I may be the woman who thinks too much but I need answers. Is seaweed-based tomato feed *plant* food, and therefore bad? Might too many slug-repelling nitrogen-rich tea-leaves actually weaken my plants and make them prey? Will corrugated-cardboard glue contaminate my compost? If I trust the *Guardian* to use soy-based ink, can the same be said for tabloid newspapers? And, if I won't eat flowers from the window boxes at the front, why am I pretending that the house magically screens the back garden from all these fumes?

The internet has brought blight and sorrow to the world, as well as pictures of piglets on trampolines, but its greatest contribution to human happiness is that, in cyberspace, you are never alone. Just as there are websites for exchanging potty-training methods, perversions, conspiracy theories, amazing uses for bicarbonate of soda and techniques for folding origami dolphins, no horticultural interest is too niche to find an online home. Do you want graphs to illustrate the exact rate at which your plastic window box will degrade, or a thesis on the ever-growing proportion of woodchip in supermarket grow-bags, 2005 to present? Are there more anthocyanins in the 'Ben Sarek' blackcurrant than in 'Ben Connan'? Should one apply linseed oil in a horizontal or vertical direction for optimal rain-proofing, or both? What are these jumpy prawn-like little scorpions under all my pot saucers and, if they are indeed *Collembola*, or springtails, a) why does every garden publication ignore them and b) if mine are of the species whose males coax females to pick up their packets of sperm by dancing and head-butting, can I watch?

If, like me, you thirst for detail, the world is full of fellow weirdoes. The first time I ever looked online for advice, in less than a minute I had found my soul mates, in the online forum of a British gardening magazine. We are all anonymous. There are different chat rooms for specialist needs, such as polytunnels or wine-making and also circles, private or public, where the most esoteric interests are discussed. From time to time one of us sends out a jiffy bag, filled with little packets; there are legal pitfalls to this but we keep our identities to ourselves.

LET'S ALL MOVE TO THE COUNTRY

Among the bittersweet joys of visiting family, only marginally eased by alcohol or selective deafness, the local paper offers a welcome diversion. It, and you, may have changed superficially but its heart is the same as before. Whip through the bus-shelter vandalism dramas, the interpretative dance performances and the bridge club's Bring and Share supper; turn, if you are not totally enfeebled, to the property section and behold the world that could be yours.

Should you go for the four-bed Edwardian villa with tennis court and solarium, or the isolated Highlands ex-hotel with award-winning spa, priced low for quick sale? The barn, the bungalow, the lighthouse? Anything, anywhere, would be bigger than your pitiful urban sardine tin and, better still, you would have land.

To the frustrated city gardener, the amount of unused space in this over-populated and badly planned country is agonising. Think of the potatoes one could grow on that traffic island. Look at that whole windowsill without any pots on it; someone should tell them. Why are there no tomatoes in your conservatory; are you mad? Have you spoken to Grandma about moving Fluffy's grave and planting raspberries there instead?

As for the country: why don't they do something with it? Not the careful gardens with two or three sheds each but the deeper countryside where, around so many houses, there is land everyone ignores. If we town-dwellers had all this room to spare, would we leave it as a wilderness of cash and carry dog-food sacks, laminated bookshelves, trailer wheels and bramble?

Of course not. It would be planted up with Jerusalem artichokes and garlic and kiwi vines by the weekend. We would be grateful for every centimetre.

So why don't we move there, and do it?

There's work, of course, and schools, and all the Vietnamese restaurants, art-house cinemas and conceptual art which we never have quite enough time to visit. Yet that isn't all. The real reason, I think, is fear. We yearn for space, but what would we do with it? If we are truly avid and obsessed and our available area were to increase, how would we ever make ourselves come indoors again?

Besides, to those of us brought up with streetlights and sirens, townies to the polluted bone, the country, even for a weekend, is an alarming place. By day we invent excuses to go to the shops, or shop, to survey the range of fudge; by night, we are frightened by the small violent deaths of furred creatures, the infinite darkness, the wind-lashed bus shelters past which no bus comes. We are too lazy for long rural walks; is there any point, without other people's front windows to peer into? Our chief interest in birds is in eating them, stir-fried; pubs intimidate us. We miss our little pets, our tired neighbours, the cramped container plants whose every shoot and leaf we know so intimately. After a couple of days of spiders and tea rooms, our smallholding yearnings are crushed. Besides, a really obsessively tended garden in the city is rare and therefore interesting. In a village, if everyone else had one, who would care about ours?

ON SAFARI

It is eleven o'clock at night, or midnight, or even later. I am tired after a long day of appointments and public transport; after one look at their delicious supper of grilled sardines and rice and greens, the children demand cheese toasties. There are still bills to pay and books to read but who knows what acts of destruction are taking place at this very moment? The fate of innocent parsley and basil lies in my hands; I know my duty.

My little armoury waits in the vegetable rack by the back door: the torch, Vanquisher of Batteries; a close-fitting glove, usually left-handed, which, nimble-minded as ever, I simply force on to my right hand; and an empty flowerpot.

'I'll be up soon,' I call as, quietly, I close the back door and hurry outside.

Sometimes we have friends for dinner: we often do and, besides, someone needs to eat all that chicory. I love my guests, mostly but, as the slugging hour approaches, I begin to fidget. I have cooked for them. The recycling is full of bottles. What more could they want? Surely I've earned a few moments of quiet, a spot of blood-letting?

But culls need planning. Without serious chemicals, the options are limited: copper bands, unfortunately not available in full-garden size; beer traps, which leads to the question of corpse disposal; the encouragement of shrews and thrushes and brown trout, which I'd like to see anyone attempt in Kentish Town; then what? One can toss them into the gardens of unpopular neighbours, but molluscs have homing instincts. Besides, slugs are too disgusting to throw. Why is this? I blame, as for most things, childhood. Snails, with their googly eyes and convenient handles, are both adorable and portable. Slugs have fewer fans: that slime, the inexorable slither. Grudgingly, I admire their variousness; whereas my garden snails merely range from vast chalky pensioners, possibly edible, to spiral-shaped shiny brown grains, slugs encompass every size and colour: small firm ones like black leather; minute glistening brown ones; mustard-coloured buggers the length of a thumb; mighty leopard slugs, 15 centimetres of grey speckled slime, on which I pounce like a lioness spotting her prey. I find them by the hundred but, however much you may try to interest me in their seasonal aggression, their vestigial shells and cannibalistic tendencies and saddle-shaped mantles, they have another feature about which I'm much more excited: they can't resist citrus peel.

And this is convenient because we are, as a family, world-class satsuma eaters. We put lemon juice on everything, always eat oranges in front of *The X-Files* and recently discovered pomelos; only kumquats are safe. The quantities of peel we produce is colossal yet the compost-worms don't like it, so imagine the gusto with which I hurl it from the back step on to the beds, like a wedding guest with inappropriate confetti. A couple of hours later, I have only to follow the gleam of torchlight on slug slime; there they are gorging on orange-pith, and vengeance is mine.

But what happens next? Do I spear, or salt, or slice, or stamp? I would love to tell you but, unfortunately, I can't. My family is curious about my slaying methods; I have always refused to tell them and this has become a matter of principle. They have begged and blackmailed but to divulge the truth would be to lose the only power I still have. Other people retain their mystique in marriage by not shaving their legs in front of their beloved; this is my equivalent.

This murderousness may be genetic. My mild-mannered father, who cried when our guinea pig, Fido, died, and chats to his dog in a language of his own devising, finds the mere existence of pigeons more than he can stand. The gentlest coo anywhere near his house makes him incandescent. If he had a gun license, there would be carnage: he is a short-sighted man. However, as long as it remains possible for a gentle septuagenarian academic to amass an arsenal of fluorescent, plastic, pump-action, multi-barrelled water pistols, no bird can call itself safe.

Luckily for us all, he hunts only by day. Every corner of the night-time garden is booby-trapped with thorns, logs, unexpected corners and, however carefully we high-step across the beds and round the containers, rending our garments, crushing fragile perennials, our prey so often evades us. The bamboo canes are never quite the sturdy handholds we had hoped; that pile of brittle, yet extremely hard, terracotta pots is ideally placed to break our fall.

Yet, when at last we stagger back into the kitchen, lightly abraded, muddied and bloodied, we are smiling. If only someone were still awake to ask, we could tell them our total: forty; seventy; one hundred and ten. Imagine if we could stuff and mount slug heads; think how we could impress our friends.

Even if one sets aside the joy of molluscicide, the garden at night is a lovely place. Cool in summer, breath-fogged in winter, its smells and surfaces are intensified by isolation: a whiff of lemon from the verbena on the step, the mysterious woodland musk of dead-nettle, the velvet secrecy of tomatillo leaves. Under the amber haze the moon reveals every textural variation of gloss or matte: neoprene, suede, satin, crocodile. Like a burglar-naturalist, nose a few centimetres from the soil, forgetting to breathe, I scan for the enemy, totally absorbed. The animal kingdom glistens in its private worlds of sex and death. I search for the dragonfly which rested for a single evening among the bay-tree suckers, finger-sized, wings like oil, thrumming as if it housed a small machine. I check on the glintingly carnivorous-looking spider which sleeps in a corner of the shed door, displaying only its shiny jet-black leg tips until, when darkness falls, it emerges: wasp-waisted, elegant, every fly's nightmare. And, several times a night, the torch beam falls upon glistening fleshly earthworms, 30 centimetres long, striped and glossy, which slither away too quickly to touch unless they are mating, their loins pressed together in slimy rapture. Then they are oblivious. Sometimes it seems as if I am hosting an orgy to which I am not invited.

Do my slug patrols have any impact? Not in the slightest. My father has another passion: biblical and classical epic films, the worse the better, featuring prophets and warriors and dramatic crowd scenes. We all know, even those of us who have been spared repeated screenings of *Demetrius and the Gladiators*, that the odds are always stacked against heroes; that they may kill one advancing phalanx, their swords black with blood, their armour all sweaty, but another will always follow, in endless rippling waves of destruction.

Nevertheless, the heroes always win. I am beginning to suspect that I never shall. The slug army keeps advancing over the bodies of its fallen comrades in unstoppable waves; besides, Carthaginian generals don't lay eggs. Yet, despite the mockery, the sleep missed, batteries drained, the toll on my poor back, the pointlessness, I can't stop going out there with my torch and galoshes, addicted to the thrill of the very slow chase.

WHY GROW FLOWERS?

I don't believe in flowers. So what are all these doing in my garden?

I'm looking at a photograph taken this time last year from the back door. Something is wrong. The calm green depths are here, every imaginable shade from sulphur to avocado to khaki, leaves frilled or feathery, felty, glaucous, curved like sails or strongly ribbed as little fish. There are all the familiar eyesores: the hardwood chair my mother bought off the back of a lorry; the sacks of seed-compost and straw mulch; the black plastic trug only a builder could love, inadequately hand-drilled for drainage, into which I have squashed at least one tomato plant too many. But what are these cherry-red tulips with clashing yellow bases doing here, blossom the colour of methylated spirits, or penny sweets, or Fanta? Who took this picture? Don't tell me that this is my garden.

Hang on, though; it does look familiar. Somehow, my sea of green has been contaminated with colour; how on earth has this happened? Then I remember: photo effects. Of course, that's it: any schoolchild with an iPhone can wreak havoc with the simplest photo, painting it sepia, adding false moustaches. Some teenaged saboteur has added ridiculous flowers to this study in monochrome.

Wait. I know the simple cup-shape of those meths-coloured flowers. Isn't that an abutilon; my abutilon? That mauve is the erysimum by the washing post. I did go slightly mad with that packet of Californian poppies, and there were those very cheap lillies. . . Wait. This is my garden; these are *my* flowers. Inadvertently, I have let decoration in.

It turns out that I wasn't quite the floral tyrant I had assumed. True, there still aren't busy lizzies, no canna and certainly no begonias but, by making space for edible flowers, and those which might woo the pollinators to my quinces and summer squashes, I seem to have been accidentally open-minded. It's like marrying for practicality, not love, and gradually discovering you actually rather like them. There, fighting for their lives among the brassicas, are calendulas in shades of neon tangerine, peach and gold; foxy-red sunflowers and deepest purple violas; sky-blue borage and dark burgundy cornflowers; the raspberry-juice and lamb's-wool strangeness of lychnis; deep-pink *Cosmos* 'Sensation'; the sulphur yellow of brassicas gone to seed; a flourishing honesty; the glamorously sixteenth-century sweet pea 'Cupani', and a single dark-leaved dahlia, its petals a surprisingly Eighties hot pink.

And, on reflection, am I immune to buying bulbs, the pick 'n' mix sweets of middle age? Hardly: each year my foolishness astounds me. How did I convince myself that among the laboriously transplanted purslane seedlings and shallow, hungry, perennial roots and dahlia tubers and self-seeded annuals and just-about-overwintered radicchio, there is space to spare in any direction, let alone 10 centimetres down? Last year's bulbs lie barely below the surface, quaking as my fingers dig ever closer. Will I never halt the annual cycle of needing more pots, buying more compost to fill the pots, buying more plants to use up the compost and then needing more pots for all those plants and on and on to the last syllable of recorded time or bankruptcy, whichever comes first?

I feel compelled to sow coriander seeds immediately; bare-rooted soft fruit bushes look at me accusingly until I've bunged them in the soil. When it comes to bulbs, I find it hard to summon much enthusiasm. It's almost a relief to find that those horrible pink and green tulip bulbs have rotted in their paper bags. Planting flowers is what normal gardeners do but I have never been good at pretending to be normal. I buy pansy seed, and let it dessicate. Given the choice between almost-instant salad rocket and the neurotic requirements of the Himalayan blue poppy, the scratchy dirty pink of a common chive versus the spectacular but inedible fireworks of *Allium* 'Globemaster', prettiness is no match for possible food. Besides, vegetables are wonderful. Give me fifty shades of green over pastels, Turner over Constable, dark hair over blonde, novels over magazines, corduroy over velvet. Let others keep the pastel hell of alstroemeria; I'm perfectly happy over here, thanks, contemplating this blistered, inky, elephant-knee-textured beauty, black kale.

ENTERTAINING

The nights are growing warmer, lighter. My slugging now requires a degree of stealth lest the neighbours, entertaining guests on their balconies, notice my crashing about and start treating me as a local highlight. And, every year, the same guilt and anxiety assails me; shouldn't we be doing the same?

There is, I have been told, repeatedly, room for several guests, if slender, in this garden. The table has a light above it, my friends cry, prettily shaded by that ridiculous canopy of tomatillo and bean leaves. This terracotta saucer is fine as an ashtray; if we could just move the sacks of compost and seed trays and trowels and scissors and these new plants (I thought you said you didn't have room for more plants) on this bench – it *is* a bench, isn't it? – couldn't we just have a drink out there?

No, we can't. Other gardeners have potting benches, ingeniously fashioned from side tables and butchers' blocks, if not purpose-built oiled oak with a zinc top. My table has to multi-task: plant life covers the surface; a thicket of kindling lies beneath it, seasoning for the winter, with teetering stacks of plant pots, a tin bath I mean to make into a pond and a novelty elephant-shaped watering can, with limited usefulness but a sweet trunk. Most of the house's contents end up here: paperclips unbent to pin down strawberry runners; biros for dibbing; chopsticks for seedling staking; corks; small bags of hair; my late grandmother's lemon-reamer, repurposed as a cane-topper. Is there not an argument – no, wait – for moving the entire kitchen outside?

It's not as if I have time for socialising. Has no one else noticed that, among the wealth of summer squash blossom, splayed buttercup-yellow flowers the size of one's hand, barely any are female? It isn't difficult to tell: the male flower lacks the maternal bulge at the base of the calyx. Its purpose is to sit there, looking handsome, waiting for a hoverfly or bee to enter its golden depths and take the pollen from its three grainy oval anthers. I fear that this is not going to be a good summer. I check every morning; when a female flower does appear I snap into action like an overinvolved harem assistant, wrenching the male organ from within its flower and running over to plunge it into the female, up as far as the waiting stigma, then watching the fruit for hints of swelling.

The signs aren't good. I have been knitting tiny bonnets for months. Is the problem too much rain or not enough? The wrong kind of bee? Something has to work: pictures of sexy courgettes in flower? Should I try flattering lighting?

ACHILLES

Nostalgia has a taste. Children's books are lessons in greed; I have never forgotten the bakery in *The Elephant and the Bad Baby*, Kenny Bear's pancakes and maple syrup in Richard Scarry's aptly named *Best Word Book Ever*, the sweet sharp juice of the Giant Peach, even the stomach-aching salami-and-lollipop bounty of *The Very Hungry Caterpillar*. We're trained up in the idea of feasting, of scoffing unlimited by sharing or self-restraint. But, sadly, there are few chances for real-life gorging, unless you are a small child, alone, in a strawberry patch.

Strawberries are compulsory for British gardeners: it is unpatriotic not to grow them. I did try. I included a couple of sun-warmed 'Pegasus' and 'Honeoye' in an extremely small home-grown fruit salad; nobody noticed. Perhaps the trouble was greed; if, rather than excitedly coaxing them to make new plants, I'd chosen one or two to act as brood mares and nipped off the runners of the others, they might have had the energy to fruit. I could even have grown them dangling prettily from pots on a windowsill, as if in a fairy story, if only I were less messy, and more organised. I am clearly at fault; it is just a question of identifying my crime.

Until then, my solution is wild strawberries: tiny, modest of yield, taxonomically nightmarish, tasting like heaven. *Fragaria vesca*, which spread on runners like tame strawberries, are also known as woodland strawberries or *fraises des bois*, as opposed to *Fragaria alpina*, alpine strawberry, whose fruits are technically longer and thinner and are spread by seed not runners. One taste and nobody cares; *Fragaria vesca* are the Ur-strawberry, the Platonic ideal of fruit. If they were any bigger, humans would die of pleasure. And, because only one or two are ever ripe at once, questions of yield are easy to ignore. You simply put this morning's harvest in your mouth, or pass it furtively to an exceptionally favoured loved one and, next day, you can poke around again among the little plants, ready for new riches.

One summer evening when I was a little girl, during the hours between primary school and fish-fingers when time stretched like toffee, I wandered to the bottom of the garden to investigate the foxgloves and Welsh poppies;

in my uniform of white and blue cotton dress and white crochet-effect acrylic socks, I must have looked like a little missionary. And there, alone, among the bumblebees, I discovered wild strawberries, and a terrible dilemma.

I ate a few, then a few more. How had my omniscient parents overlooked them? Had I been a tortoise life would have been simple. Tortoises love strawberries; Gerald Durrell's Achilles in *My Family and Other Animals* 'would become positively hysterical at the mere sight of them, lumbering to and fro, craning his head to see if you were going to give him any, gazing at you pleadingly with his tiny boot-button eyes'. The problem was that I was not Achilles but an obedient human child, too scared of authority and pitifully adult-pleasing to keep this bounty for myself. So I knelt, pulled the hem of my skirt to form a rudimentary basket, filled it with berries and, proud of my unusual ingenuity, stood up.

Stupid child. My mother, I knew as I looked down at the pulpy mess of strawberry juice on what had been my lap, would be enraged; I had read enough books to know that staining meant trouble. Tearfully I hurried indoors; then I had a brilliant idea. I would bundle up my dress in the washing machine! She would wash it without realising!

A masterful plan, with one fatal flaw. Whether or not my mother was furious when she discovered the damp ball of strawberry cotton, I have no idea. I had already sent myself to my room without any supper.

MIDSUMMER

'A high blank wall ... figured over with the patches
that please a painter, repaired breaches, crumblings of
plaster, extrusions of brick that had turned pink with
time; and a few thin trees, with the poles of certain
rickety trellises, were visible over the top.'

Henry James, *The Aspern Papers*

THE FALLACY OF MINT

Among the many outlandish lies to which we gardeners are heir is the concept of Mint As Pest. How can this be? It would be like having a plague of Thai basil, a torrent of chervil; for anyone even slightly interested in food, too much mint can only be a blessing.

All you need is a little imagination. We Brits don't monkey around with mint, thanks very much. We believe that its proper place is suspended in gelatinous sweetened vinegar, soaked in Pimm's or distilled, powdered, pressed and formed into a small hard lozenge with a central hole. The colder parts of Europe are just as bad: parsley fiends, lovage worshippers, they don't understand it either. But look elsewhere: the deep meaty beef-shank *phos* of Vietnam, the herb plates of Iran, Lebanese yoghurt sauce with sumac and cinnamon; the mixed bitter greens of Aegean islands; *salsa verde* and Moroccan tisanes; Goan coconut chutney; mojitos and caipirinhas and juleps. There is so much potential.

Yet, although I would adore to be overrun with spearmint, Moroccan mint, peppermint, apple mint like silken lamb's ears, mints ginger, or pineapple, or variegated, or simply garden, it never happens. At first, as in all things horticultural, I did what I was told. I worked hard to restrain their profligate urges, planting them in plastic pots with the base sawn off. Where was the promised flourishing, before the roots became choked? I seemed to keep missing it. Next I tried rebellion, burying eau-de-cologne mint, the embittered aunt of Parma violets, and chocolate mint, which I hoped would be like farming After Eights, straight into the beds then standing back, expecting a minty wave of greenery. Now, several years later, I have nothing but spindly garden-mint sproutings and, unfortunately, a lifetime's supply of eau-de-cologne mint which tastes utterly disgusting.

Parsley is notoriously difficult to germinate; coriander must prefer the tropics; dill quickly flops; there is no such thing as sufficient French tarragon and, only by deciding to treat thyme as an annual, have I and 'Silver Posie' reached an understanding. But mint's recalcitrance is an offence. I'm giving it my last shot: the deep curved-bottomed metal container, like an industrial-sized pestle, which was left behind by the garden's previous owners because it rolls on the brickwork unless creatively propped. It is deep and wide and shaded, heaped with the finest compost my brindled worms can generate and, despite lavish encouragement and my knocking a single triangular drainage hole through the rust, everything planted in it suffers.

I am certain that the mint will grow in it like Topsy. This year, definitely, we shall be overcome.

THE SMELL OF HOME

Failing mint, imagine having too much garlic.

In the fertile, if occasionally murderous, farmland of the Transcarpathian mountains, where chestnuts and apples peel themselves, mushrooms leap dewily into one's apron, peppers dry on every doorframe and *nem tudom* plums from beside the River Tisza simmer themselves into ambrosial jam, my grandmother and her seven sisters learned to cook. They cooked as grandmothers are supposed to: without fuss, or fashion, or constraint and with extraordinary quantities of garlic. This was Transylvania, after all.

As a result, I believe that garlic is generally the answer. Like soffrito or an Indian tarka, it brings savoury food closer to perfection; softening onions are sweetly delicious, the smell of bacon could break almost anyone but, for me, food begins to smell right only when garlic arrives.

Yet I can't grow it. It is no use planting any old cloves in midwinter and expecting plenty. After cooking my way through twenty or thirty miniature bulbs, barely the size of jumbo marbles, each clove a puny fingernail, I decided to invest in official purpose-grown bulbs at a couple of pounds a pop. But how to choose between the softneck 'Iberian Wight', 'Picardy Wight' and 'Solent Wight', and the curly-flower-stalk-producing and frankly more glamorous-sounding 'Carcassonne', 'Lautrec' and 'Bohemian Rose' hardnecks? Paralysed by indecision, I missed the moment.

Luckily, I grow every other type of garlickage I can lay my hands on: garlic chives, sometimes called Chinese chives for extra excitement; society garlic; *Tulbaghia violacea* 'Fairy Star', of which my favourite and most niche catalogue, from the Edulis nursery, lists an almost unbearably exciting eighteen other kinds; *Allium hookeri* 'Zorami', which has white flowers and cookable stems; and two different tussocks of wild garlic, a broad-leafed type, which uprooted itself and accidentally jumped into a carrier bag when I was casually walking along a Welsh river bank, and another, resembling narrow-leaved snowdrops, rescued from beneath scaffolding. I have always been very proud of this rare allium; I even put a photo of it online, to the surprise of a local gardening journalist, who explained that it's actually a three-cornered leek, which grows wild in every driveway and alley between here and Camden Town.

Yet, when I discover those familiar strappy leaves among the crocosmia, do I pick them? I wish I dared; I am too frightened of running out. So every year I grow more, tending them lovingly, gently rubbing and sniffing their delicious stinky sap, then come indoors and cook with pesticide-reared supermarket Chinese garlic while my grandmother and her seven sisters spin in their garlicky graves.

PLEASE DON'T
MENTION PURPLE

My *Tulbaghia*'s insipid sherbet-pink blossom does little for me, but there are some flowers – a really extravagant parrot tulip in full Sarah Bernhardt faint, for example, or the strawberry-bronze buds of *Epimedium* 'Amber Queen', or a magnolia tree in bloom – which move even my philistine heart. It's very odd. A delicately veined cat, a green and pink woman, would repel us, so why do we find flowers beautiful? Is our attraction to them merely primal: flowers mean (usually) fertile soil, fertile soil means fat herbivores, herbivores mean dinner? It makes sense if, very gradually, we evolved to think of these indicators as objectively attractive. The odd thing is that nobody knows. Pollen deposits have been found in burial sites over a hundred thousand years old, when only the most rudimentary garden centres existed. Were our ancestors having a decorative moment, or did flowers appeal to their sense of curiosity about the world or, as some psychologists currently believe, have flowers themselves evolved to make us find them attractive, as they have with insects, in order to increase their chances of pollination?

We do know that pollinators' colour preference is innate. Bees prefer yellow, blue or violet flowers while hoverflies favour white or yellow, just as some pollinators, depending on their physiology, prefer flat flowers, like umbellifers, or short trumpets, such as salvia, and still others need long tunnel-shaped blossom: honeysuckle, foxgloves. But how does it works for humans? Why is one person's cottage garden idyll another's sappy chocolate-box hell?

Just as a tiny girl-child may state a preference for pink, apparently instinctive yet piped directly to her brain by toy manufacturers and the publishers of terrifying infant 'magazines'; just as adults' favourite colours have personal associations, so too, as gardeners, we have to accept that we have no minds of our own. Why do some of us favour pastels, or so-called hot colours? Is an obsession with blue merely a snobbish liking for the rarer flowers, or proof of a profound affinity with the sky and sea?

Children believe in having a favourite colour. Mine, I have realised, is red, the bright true scarlet of a pillar box; as much of it as possible, on saucepans and bags and belts and scarves and shelves. My other favourites are equally primary-school; yellow, judiciously (a folder, a pair of shoes) and that intense mid-blue, known in France as Yves Klein blue, a little like the Majorelle Garden in Marrakesh. Yet my garden doesn't contain a single red rose: no scarlet cosmos or pansies or petunias for me. I don't do blue, although Eleanor Perényi's *Green Thoughts*, one of my favourite garden books, contains an elegy to blue flowers, giant delphiniums and azure Italian bugloss, anchusa and the confusingly indigo-flowered false indigo. I eschew daffodils; even my sunflowers are terracotta. So if, grudgingly, we discount the various shades of green leaf, from heuchera-lime to hellebore-black, what colours are left?

Orange is fit only for citrus fruit or festival-goers, yet I find it irresistible in the garden. On the never-ending list in my diary, certain plants keep reappearing: tangerine *Geum* 'Prinses Juliana', *Crocosmia* × *crocosmiiflora* 'Star of the East', the ruthlessly bright *Tithonia rotundifolia* and the apricotty *Dahlia* 'David Howard'. However often I try to branch out, the two flowers which spill out of every tub and corner are the Day-Glo nasturtium 'Tom Thumb' and pot marigold, the brighter the better.

As for pink: I loathe pink. Too sappy, too wishy-washy or, at the hotter end, too look-at-me yet, even when we have discounted the sweet blossoms on the quince and apricot and apple, and the allium flowers ... oh, and the sweet peas, and the lychnis, what about the rosebud-pink flush on my favourite hellebore, Walberton's Rosemary, or the pointillist frenzy of *Achillea millefolium* 'Cerise Queen', and the strawberry-pink astrantia I grow for the bees, or the rose I keep for its hips and pretend not to mind its colour?

Please don't mention purple. Despite the Jenny Joseph poem on fridges throughout Britain, it suits plums and nothing else. It is pink's pretentious older sister. Each note on its spectrum, particularly at the paler end, from cheap satin-bedspread violet to bridemaid mauve, is bad news: a shortcut to sophistication. Yes, it can be worn with dash, like the otherwise ordinary-looking man I once spotted at the British Library, whose entire outfit – tweed jacket and trousers, shirt, tie – was shades of lavender. But think of hospital waiting rooms and beauty products aimed at women. Sugary lilac and cheap blackcurrant-lozenge bad enough, but the lighter shades of purple are always a bad sign.

So what is this terrible colour doing all over my garden? I'm looking down from my study window and the garden is a sea of it: the indubitably lavender lavender; my flourishing but sadly mauve abutilon, its petals like those of its neighbouring geranium 'Rozanne' but softer; the thuggish off-blue potato vine *Solanum crispum* 'Glasnevin'; scabious and alliums and aquilegia and fragrant but sugary-looking lilac; catmint and all the other mints; *Erysimum* 'Bowles Mauve'. The clue was in the name, yet still I bought it. If there had been an amethyst-coloured variety of *Trachelosper-mum jasminoides* I'd have snapped it up too. Even my proud new acquisition from Beth Chatto, *Verbena officinalis* var. *grandiflora* 'Bampton', with its slim bruised-purple leaves and murky stems, has tiny mauve starry flowers; was it the Curse of Famous Gardens, the mistaken belief that what works in a great garden might add beauty to one's own? Did you know that mallow is the source of the word 'mauve'? I'm probably about to buy one of those, too. However often my instinct draws me towards a darker and more interesting shade – the brooding Oxfordy checks of the snake's head fritillary and the liquorice sheen of *Tulipa* 'Queen of the Night', the glow of *Clematis* 'Polish Spirit' or the tiny but alluring *Salvia nachtvlinder*, its petals a rich Venusian-dusk deep purple – they disappear in the tumult that is my garden, while the mauve elbows its way to centre stage.

The answer, as with so much else, is vegetables. Look at this burgundy bull's blood leaf, a sliced Chioggia beetroot's cream and fuchsia, the mimeograph violet of a 'Cosse Violette' flower. Let me at a really perky bunch of Russian kale, smoked green glass and raspberry, or the venous tinge of radicchio darkening in the frost. Clearly, I am unfit to choose garden flowers but, when it comes to vegetables, I'm an artist; one has only to look.

PERIL

The house is awash with potting compost and seed packets. Frail seedlings and their potted-out cousins, some on the verge of middle age, cover the garden table, beside tragic parsley rescued from nurseries and a saxifrage from the farmers' market because I sense that I am on the verge of falling for alpines. The so-called cold frame is heaving with overwintered banana-plant children and mystery purchases for which I failed to find homes last year. I have an introduction to write, which means reading six long novels very quickly, but the garden is calling to me: a thicket of tangled life.

This morning, when I step outside to pick berries for breakfast, a bird is singing in the end neighbours' maddeningly unreachable apple-tree. It's a bright clear day; the sun is already well above the light-blocking clutter of ivy and honeysuckle in the corner. Balancing on the plain terracotta tile and the blue agapanthus tile, I reach five warm sweet-sharp raspberries, one matte and winey and unfit to share; three blackcurrants and twelve redcurrants; four wild and one tame strawberry; two rather dry but almondy Juneberries from my fading amelanchier; and a single 'Hinnomaki Red' gooseberry. I will share them with my family, I think, nobly. But for once, as I gaze around me, absent-mindedly eating the currants and delighting in their tartness, the chalky mouth-drying seeds, I am barely distracted by the jobs I should be doing, inside or out. Today I will play truant; I am going to the plant fair.

I live for this fair. Its spring and autumn dates are the anchors of my year; close friends may be getting married, to each other, but, sadly, I have other plans. Yet, unlike many other gardeners, I have never visited the Chelsea or Hampton Court Flower Shows. I don't dare. How do they control themselves? I'd be like a child in the Swizzels-Matlow sweet factory with a credit card: all those unusual plants, those compellingly pointless contraptions? Besides, those fairs have a grandeur which alarms the foreign peasant in me; I fear being trampled under a stampede of Prince Charles enthusiasts. I long to go, I will go, if someone will come with me.

This local fair, however, is perfect: it fits into a primary-school playground with space left over for a game of Stuck-in-the-Mud. There is, however, no time for frivolity. The lugubrious stallholders in their monogrammed fleeces have work to do, despite their persistent coughs; their customers are focused, ardent. Other than cursory small talk with acquaintances from last year and opaque interrogations – 'But are you quite sure that the stems are fully lax? With absolutely no inner shading?' – they circulate in silence, like oligarchs at a jewellery auction, comparing the stock with the studied casualness of those who are prepared to kill for what they desire.

My favourite stall, on your right as you enter, is managed by the fair's organisers: pink-cheeked elderly enthusiasts who could quite easily run the Pentagon, if they could spare the time. I'm always a bit too friendly, drawn to their soothing English wholesomeness, their dazzling propagating expertise but, to them, I'm just another idiot, mixing up pelargoniums and geraniums.

'Will this,' I ask, raising my voice over the rain drumming on their portable gazebo, 'grow bigger than—'

'Margery, do *you* think it's an *aureopunctata urbium*?' says the one in the blue anorak, pouring yet more tea. 'I think we had a *dentata*, didn't we, under the table? Or was that one of Peter's *arendsii*, you never know with him. You might find,' she confides, 'that its leaves are a little less pinking-sheared than the *rotundifolia*, if that's what you're after, but it grows horribly well in my garden; I've been pulling them up for weeks. Actually it's a good pinky-white, much softer than the 'Kewensis'. I've probably overpriced it. What shall we say, fifty pee?'

'Sorry,' I say. 'I just meant, is it a tree or a flower?'

The other customers know what they are doing. They may look like lay nuns or retired surveyors, but they will rip your arm off if you accidentally brush against their newly acquired *Hemerocallis middendorffii esculenta*. They will give you advice, too; show them a one-litre *Salvia* × *sylvestris* 'Blauhügel' for £8.50 beside a 23-centimetre *Salvia* × *sylvestris* 'Mainacht' at £5.85 and they will know with Linnaean precision which is the better grown, the prettier shape, the stronger hue. I wander cluelessly among them, drawn by the least word overheard, the tersest label: 'extremely rare'; 'admired'; 'little known'. Over-alert, over-stimulated, I find everything helplessly moving: the handwritten labels on the plum jam sold at the trestle by the entrance, the carrier bags of plants waiting untended for their owners.

In autumn, fortunately, part of the space is occupied by a bulb stall; it does not trouble me, much. Extremely unusual tulip bulbs, in paper bags like buns from an old-fashioned bakery, don't really count, do they? In spring, I can usually manage to avoid the cheery man in the poacher's jacket, whose approachable cottagey-sounding nursery is, I suspect, a front for a cruel Dutch battery farm where baby perennials are reared at unnatural speed. Yet these small measures of self-preservation are drops in the ocean of my longing. I circulate, agonise and, at last, allow myself to approach the furthest corner, just beyond the painted hopscotch template: the Edulis unusual edibles stall.

They're not even all edible. The centre of the trestle table, for more balanced browsers, is dominated by rare Chinese epimediums, a purple lilyturf, *Liriope muscari* 'Variegata', and the enticingly named false plumbago. In any other context I could ignore their relentlessly inedible evergreen leaves, their temporary flowers and pointless little rhizomes. Yet so strong is the lure of the unusual that, even as I vow to save my remaining money, I find myself weirdly drawn to them, like iron filings attempting to slip past a magnet.

And, even if I decide there is a place in my heart, if not my garden, for a 'Rose Madder' dusky cranesbill, when it comes to the ends of the table, where the edibles cluster, I am lost. How could anyone resist a Himalayan may apple? A Japanese bitter lemon, or the *Schisandra chinensis*, Wu Wei Zi, a white-flowered deciduous climber 'said to aid night vision'? Its berries can be eaten dried or fresh, which makes them virtually dual-purpose; my need is pressing. I can't go home without it, despite having found a note in my bag saying NOT SCHISANDRA STAUTONIA NB, whose meaning now eludes me. But what about the strawberry 'Malling Pandora', said to be hugely productive; wouldn't this be the solution to my insufficient-strawberry shame? Say I were to buy both ... hang on, hadn't I planned on an earth chestnut, *Bunium bulbocastanum*, because it's both pretty and more peculiar than mere potatoes? And then how about sorrel 'Silver Shield' to replace the plain green buckler-leafed sorrel which, in the moronic first dawn of my gardening life, I allowed to flourish and then tore up because I thought it was making the blueberries unhappy? I can't buy five plants, absolutely not, particularly given that I'm pretending to myself that the bag at my feet, already containing a deliciously dark sedum 'Purple Emperor' and, if we're honest, a passionflower and a tiny pulsatilla and yet another thyme, broad-leaved this time, is nothing to do with me. Oh help: lime mint, which ... yes, actually tastes of lime. And late last night with Mark Diacono's *New*

Kitchen Garden, hadn't I set my heart on a Chinese cedar, 'one of the tastiest of the tree leaves'? This is a disaster. Isn't that an aronia, which allegedly is wildly underrated, with delicious berries and bright autumn foliage, the one unusual fruit bush everyone urgently needs? (I've forgotten the aronia I bought last year; still confined to its pot, as likely to produce an edible berry as I am.) And a real, cutting-grown Daubenton's kale and, my God, is that mad pompom pink and green hop flower seriously *Origanum rotundifolium*, I've needed that for months, and you're saying that the buffalo currant is both productive *and* delicious? Then surely that's a must?

It's all very well for these semi-professionals with space to fill. Some of us don't even know how much space we do have. At night, in my dreams, my garden grows immense and fabulous: 'Oh,' I think, rounding a beech hedge, 'I'd forgotten about that vast grassy amphitheatre. And a meadow! There's space to plant those grape hyacinths, after all.' Waking is always a disappointment but, even when fully conscious, I seem unable to get my garden's puny dimensions into my head.

Is there really no space for a hazel, for sticks and nuts; what about a cherry plum? It only grows to 3 metres, and most of those are up. What about a really tiny potting shed. A hill? A hillock. A minuscule herd of deer?

Wait. What is this Japanese couple discussing over my shoulder? Wasabi? A wasabi plant? There's only one left but, if I move stealthily closer, and they decide to go for the golden hosta instead, poor fools, which the man is angling for, I could easily—

I REMEMBER NOTHING

Most people have a memory for names, or faces. I have neither. My father once forgot my mother's name when he was about to introduce her; he loses everything, forgets everything and, because he is brainy-seeming, we call it absent-mindedness. Like him, I wander about in a cloud of unknowing, hoping for the best. The other day, after paying for petrol, I crossed the forecourt, opened the door, sat down in the driver's seat and started talking before realising that the paintwork was not black but green, the person in the passenger's seat was a stranger and I was sitting in the wrong car.

There isn't much I remember. Recent conversations, acquaintances, directions, enormous pieces of gossip evaporate instantaneously and new information, particularly if it has the slightest practical application, barely leaves a trace. Did I really stay in Devon this time last year? Have we met? Are you sure you told me we were moving? Really, it's a miracle I'm even upright. Yet I remember Latin.

What a privilege it is to write those words; how sad that privilege comes into it. I am lucky to have caught the last wave of compulsory Latin in English schools; one can only hope that little Romans and Neapolitans still learn it, rather having it saved for them at university, like English undergraduates suffering through *Piers Plowman*. Because, despite having had, by British Eighties standards, a marvellous education, I know very little. The taxation schemes of the Visigoths have proved entirely useless; velocity and gears remain as mysterious to me as to a spaniel, probably much more so.

But those mere four years of Latin opened worlds. For one, it gave me the vocabulary of a pre-war civil servant, saying 'pertains' or 'obdurate' or 'celerity' in perfectly ordinary conversation. More usefully, I can usually guess the meaning of English words and, even when wrong, I sound magnificently convincing. I can conduct entire conversations in pretend-Italian, simply by smiling while sticking half-remembered syllables together. I know an entire poem about Catullus's girlfriend's sparrow. But, best of all, it helps me garden.

No one knows how Latin is pronounced. My father says Veni Vidi Viki, I say Weni Weedy Weeky and, just as Shakespearean English may, or may not, have sounded much like American English does today, nobody has a clue which, if either, is correct. Merely knowing this fact gives one a certain power. Plant names can be daunting, clotted and foreign: which of us has not had their pronunciation corrected, rightly or wrongly, of knautia or wistaria, let alone *Paeonia mlokosewitschii*, known by many, to save face, as Molly the Witch? But a knowledge of Latin takes the fear from a double 'ii'; it renders *Thymus pseudolanuginosus* merely woolly, *Thymus vulgaris* widespread, not vulgar, and *Fritillaria meleagris* spotted like a guinea-fowl.

And so, at last, Latin has become useful. I will never have a fraction of the knowledge of those plant-fair women, but merely knowing that *sanguinea* means blood-red, or being able to link *campanula* to bells, makes the words richer, as if the centuries between gardeners have an echo. Even better, when I have no idea what the root is, Latin has somehow paved the way for those odd words to slip into my otherwise leaky memory: ah, yes, *vincus*, I think as I pass what I've only just learned is a periwinkle; *malva, centaurea, verbascum*. I don't know the English folk names; I have no idea how they grow. But, thanks to Latin, they have meaning and resonance. I may remember nothing, but I can guess that *foetidissima* means amazingly smelly, and what could be more useful than that?

LATE SUMMER

'Where all is stone around, blank wall and hot
pavement, how precious seems one shrub, how lovely
an enclosed and planted spot of ground!'

Charlotte Brontë, *Villette*

UGH

T. S. Eliot was wrong about many things, including April. It isn't the cruellest month: crueller by far is right now, the long dog days of unflattering skimpy garments, office sandwiches on sticky park benches, shouty outdoor drinkers and tattoos aired in public. For those of us with pale blue freckled skin, lovers of stews and wearers of jumpers, deep summer is a time of woe.

Only the garden offers consolation. That cramped fumy journey home from work will float away like dandelion fluff if you can slip outside and spend ten minutes among the greenery, the soft petals and rich earthy scents, tending your plants. That, at least, is the theory. In truth, for most of us, particularly if we grow fruit and vegetables, the garden in summer is not a restful place. Everything needs to be staked and inspected and harvested and, most of all, watered, to avoid fallen fruits, bolting, salad leaves like withered skin. Almost nothing in this garden of containers and tiny spaces can cope with drought. Rhubarb is hardy and trouble-free, provided that one waters it even if it's raining; gardening journalists recommend *Trachelospermum jasminoides* for any environment, which is why I planted mine against the wall, among the Japanese anemone and hellebores, where the ivy blocked rain from its roots so effectively that it almost died. Keeping it alive is simple, now that I have learned once in a while to turn the hosepipe to a trickle, insert it carefully in the crook of a viburnum pruning and then, after the usual rearings-up and swishings and sprayings, running back to reattach the connector to the tap, rootling around the undergrowth for lost plastic sprockets, unkinking and repinioning. By now completely drenched and fully aware that the least change in water pressure will send the hose head once more leaping free, I go inside for dinner, soothed by the knowledge that my *Trachelospermum*, at least, is comfortable.

We are so lucky; rain in this country is, generally, lavish. We may hoard it, but only to give the blueberries a change from their usual breakfast of calcium and magnesium carbonates, fluoride and chlorinated hormones. We may try to reduce our tap-water dependence (me, a hosepipe, a full bathtub two floors up and a rudimentary knowledge of siphoning; it was not a happy combination) but the effort is rarely more than token. As summer progresses, those of us with too many containers start to grow anxious. Which will come first: autumn rain, or sheer exhaustion?

Like swans moulting and growing fresh flight-feathers in summer, or trees shedding their leaves, gardeners live according to an annual cycle:

a) acquiring too many seeds
b) needing more receptacles
c) panicking
d) retreating.

This is the season for panic. Around this time of year, what container-grower is not moved almost to tears by her folly? It seems only last week that, in torrents of rain, I was eyeing plastic florists' buckets, still containing flowers, at the stall at Camden tube, and liberating disposable fruit crates from outside the corner shop because my seedlings needed a halfway house before the next pot size was free. Then the weather turned, for the so-called better; I look at this bedlam, this cobbled-together chaos of wire baskets and fibre pots and plastic tubs and wine boxes and waxed-paper cups and punnets, the dry soil, the plants feebly waving their wilted leaves and foresee disaster. How will anything survive? And how is it that, every year, I vow to reduce the number of containers and hence my watering-can hell, yet the numbers have grown? Do they . . . reproduce?

I own two watering cans, both plastic, both unattractively bright, yet possessing a demonic ability to blend into the surrounding scant foliage at the moment you most need them. When filled, despite being of different capacities, they weigh the same: much too much. As for the pots, I have just counted more than seventy, excluding all the temporary seedling homes, the ten succulents and house plants holidaying outside, and the twenty containers at the front. This would be bad enough in a sane garden, where plants of similar needs are grouped together; here, like a terrible dinner party, each pot wants something radically different from its neighbour. Take the back door-step; the lemon verbena and rose pelargonium, surprisingly tough, have only to be kept from total desiccation. However, the experimental lemongrass in the next-door pot cohabits with a black grape, triumphantly grown by me from a stolen cutting; and a 'Flamenco' strawberry; what I had thought was a tiny *Geranium* 'Samobor' (Beth Chatto's *Handbook* disagrees), which I am nursing through a tricky adolescence; a solitary 'Carouby de Maussane' purple-flowered pea; a sickly 'Diva' cucumber. You see the problem? It's like trying to home-school when one child yearns romantically for poetry and Greek; the next requires a basic grounding in home economics; the third is appallingly dyslexic but naturally mathematical; and the fourth is fit only for a lifetime of circus skills at vegan alternative-music festivals.

Sage requires Mediterranean hillsides. Lettuce needs water. Again and again, distracted by the need to use every centimetre of space to the utmost, I ignore these basic facts. The pots have become so entangled, so unhealthily co-dependent, that even if the fig Pat gave me, the hardy Japanese ginger, *Zingiber mioga*, the tomatillo with its felty leaves and interesting useless fruits, the countless failing sprigs of thyme and luxuriant nasturtiums, the 'Black Krim' tomato and the nameless tomato I bought from the deli ('Call it Enzo!' cried the owners, ignoring my white-knuckled grip on the counter as I begged for varietal information) ... even if they all were in individual pots and could be watered separately, they are entwined with the beans whose stems wrap intimately around each shoot, hauling themselves towards the trellis that I have cleverly placed just out of reach.

Watering is a delicate process, which non-gardeners fail to understand.

'Why,' ask the unwary, 'not save yourself some time? Give them a going-over with the hosepipe and let them get on with it? Treat them mean!'

Arrant ignorance: I deal with it every day. Of course it *is* possible to use the hose on the sturdier plants, if one turns the regulator extremely low and adjusts the flow constantly between haze and torrent, as if one were a Roman house-slave nervously running the Emperor's bath. If one achieves the perfect intensity of spray (soft summer rain) one can even water many seedlings at once, although there will be casualties and quick work is needed to rescue newborn leaves which have been knocked astray.

Watering a garden like this is an art, a craft, a science. There should be medals. After a long tiring day, as you contemplate your million pots, you may have a moment of weakness, lean achily against a wall. If you are fortunate, someone will shout from the kitchen, 'want me to have a go?'

Exhausted, you agree. You will regret it. Like a firefighter they stand there, rather proud of their skilful hose work, crushing tender stems with reckless spurting while leaving the thirstiest plants, the raspberries and mint, barely moistened.

'I've finished,' they announce, while your teabag is still steeping. Never mind; go back outside and praise them; they are brutish ignoramuses but you may yet need their help. Then, unobtrusively, stick your finger in the soil: it will be wet for a millimetre, no more.

Containers dry out so quickly. Only with a watering can (such a quaint, Thomas-Jeffersonesque name) can one ensure that the water truly reaches the roots, instead of pooling like quicksilver on the dusty soil surface before trickling over the lip of the container and filling the saucer, convincing the careless locum-gardener that the plant has drunk its fill. Proper, individual watering is like a home visit by a kindly family doctor: is all well? Are there interesting sicknesses: magnesium issues? A problem with boron? How are they in themselves? Just as children once thought about the wellbeing of their hamsters and now consider their electronic pets, one needs to check on each plant. And so watering even this laughably tiny garden is a slow, but delicious-smelling, process. When I can no longer lug a watering can, I will totter outside with a milk bottle, a mug, a thimble-full. It is a chore, but I could not live without those whiffs of cool mint and spicy tomato leaves. The garden and I are keeping each other alive.

So please, please don't mention the summer holidays. All over the country on golden afternoons, one may hear, if one listens carefully, the sound of anxious gardeners digging in their heels. How can we trust the neighbour or the house-sitter? We'd be counting the days until our return; wouldn't a fortnight on the back step be almost as good as going abroad? Here's a recipe for lemonade; nowadays one can buy Soleros and Magnums in multipacks. Isn't there an argument, a very strong one, for staying at home?

We never win. Nobody understands us. They think it's exciting to lie in someone else's garden, being scratched by their prickly lawn and stung by their hornets. But my 'Oregon Spring' tomatoes are ripening. My 'Ophelia' aubergine, after hand-pollinating and careful feeding, always remembering to keep a saucer of water at its foot to promote humidity, is on the verge of producing an actual fruit. I can't admit this in public but please don't make me go on holiday. Even if my plants survive my absence, how will I?

ON THE FLAG

Feathered maidens; dead-heading; ever-bearing; second earlies; tilth; rod and spur: gardening is peppered with extraordinary phrases, but my favourite by far is 'on the flag'.

This should be a euphemism for periods, or a minor novel about British bureaucracy in Peshawar. Instead it is, as you almost certainly know, a term for fairly extreme tomato wilt in hot weather. Their stems floppy, leaves matt, hopelessness emanating from every stoma, they look as if they're ready for the knacker's yard; it is tempting to pull them up on the spot. Instead, it is time to rejoice. Growing tomatoes requires circus plate-spinner precision, ceaselessly balancing yield, flavour, the chance of ripening and what one of my catalogues, the Cassandra of seed merchants, calls 'the three big threats – blight, early blight and fruit cracking'. We tomato-growers will clutch at any fragment of wisdom so, when told that 'on the flag' is the best possible moment at which to water our plants, even if every instinct screams otherwise, we obey.

I love my tomato plants, a little too much. In the infinitely seductive world of vegetables, they have rare power. Merely their names are enough to quicken the pulse: 'Merveilles des Marchés', 'Black Opal', 'Harbinger', 'Cherokee Purple', 'Indigo Beauty', 'Moonglow', 'Bloody Butcher'. Those of us who are vulnerable to a really good name can be manipulated mercilessly; we'd buy ping-pong balls if the right noun and colour were combined. In some years I tried and largely failed with nine or ten different varieties, all from seed: dull pink 'Gartenperle'; impossible 'Brandywine'; the plum-shaped 'San Marzano', which in English summers tastes like moistened felt; 'Ailsa Craig', as exciting as its name. These days, sadder, wiser, I favour smaller varieties, which are more likely to ripen before the blight spores ride into town: 'Tigerella'; 'Gardener's Delight'; the great-grandchildren of Pat's 'Peacevine Cherry'; 'Broad Ripple Yellow Currant', reputedly found in a crack in a pavement in Indianapolis; excitingly dark and juicy 'Black Russian'; 'Green Zebra'; and my Dark Lady, my Belle Dame Sans Merci, 'Costoluto Fiorentino', whose heavy fruit are so deeply ribbed and mottled with green and rose that its tiny yield makes me love it even more, the caviar of vegetable fruit.

There is too much to do, and I love it. Part of the joy of tomato-growing is that one's work is never done. This is why I prefer the varieties that grow as vines or cordons, not bush tomatoes, the drearily named determinates, which quickly become a thicket of criss-crossing stems. A cordon requires effort, and plenty of it: planting the seedling deeply in its pot to encourage opportunistic roots; staking it gently; hand-pollinating every last flower; pinching out the side shoots. The smell is glorious; the prospect of warm home-grown fruit, fragrant and magnificently showy-offy, is irresistible. I do everything I'm told, except putting the side shoots in glasses of water to make more plants. I'm already drowning in plantlets; extras would push me over the edge.

Until this year it was fashionable to pick off the lower leaves once the fruit has set, to allow air to circulate and the sun to reach the cordons. Today, just after the latest round of defoliation, I read that leaves produce most of the sugar. What a fool I have been; the guilt is terrible. I had planned to coax the 'Tigerella' up a string tied to the trellis, like a well-trained boa constrictor; is that wrong now too? I can't keep up. I keep forgetting not to put broken pots at the bottom of containers, as we did until the year before last.

Sometimes I wonder if I am strong enough for this.

THE BEAUTY
OF THE SQUASHES

Much of gardening is a lie, and the biggest of all involves courgettes. In the olden days, when street urchins were polite and politicians were gentlemen, it really was possible to be self-sufficient in vegetables, provided that one adored root vegetables and could spend uninterrupted hours after work with one's sleeves rolled up. Times change. For every professional enthusiast who weighs their runner beans and blogs about their extraordinary savings, there are thousands of us whose toil produces barely enough to keep a vole in vitamins. There is probably more nutrition in the seed packets, paper and all, than in the average amateur harvest.

Still we persist. We believe the tales of glut and plenty; we struggle on. But of all the myths perpetuated by gardening publications, the most wicked is this: that, from a single courgette plant, mountains of fruit will follow.

What a colossal fib this is. I have grown perhaps twenty types of courgette in my short gardening lifetime: round, long, ridged, blackish or yellow or creamy-white, spacecraft-shaped or striped. Each was marginally more disappointing than the last. Slugs, frost, drought, sunstroke; the reasons are endless, yet I persisted, and failed, and gnashed my horticulturally inept teeth, and began again. Little humiliates the home vegetable-grower more than having to buy a courgette, in a shop, for money. It isn't right. I am coming to hate them: the subtle prickles that irritate one's hands, the strange clingy squeak that adheres to one's tooth enamel. This must stop.

However, there is a solution. I grow 'Tromboncino', one seed of which will produce an uncontrollably immense vine with comically huge fuzzy leaves and a glut, nearly, of mighty phallic bendy summer squashes. 'Tromboncino', *Zucchetta rampicante, tromba d'Albenga*: these marvellous cucurbits have many names, but are unmistakable. The fruit is like a courgette taken to extremes: a pale alien green, easily 60 centimetres long and weighing more than a cat, hanging heavily from a rampant yet beautiful vine. Better still, they look hilarious. Italian names are creative: *gemelli*, twins, for cuff-links; *cappuccino* after the confusingly not foam-topped capuchin monks. I had assumed that calling this long, bendy, swollen-ended cucurbit a trombone is meant to signify the swooping arch of the slide, or even its sound. After extensive investigations I have established that 'to trombone' is a sexual euphemism and there are, frankly, no vegetables more penis-shaped. Let us move quickly on.

I am an evangelist for this marvellous squash. Everything about it is superlative. It is easy to grow, once you have tracked down some seeds; you will feel bountiful simply by planting them, so fat and potential-stuffed do they feel. The seedlings, too, are satisfying: their plump fuzzy seed leaves, the way that the seed casing invariably sticks to a green tip, obliging you to pick it off delicately, like a loving parent with an infantile excrescence.

Soon, like any proud parent, you will be showing it to strangers, convinced that nothing of its size or grace has ever been seen before. First, there are its magnificent leaves, easily 40 centimetres across and so plentiful that, when one becomes mildewed or ragged, you can just snip it off, through its hollow stem and, once again, the plant is beautiful. Second, it is a talented mountaineer, tenacious and energetic, growing more quickly and spectacularly than any other plant I know. Save it from the slugs and it will be off, zooming up and along and over anything its vine-curly tendrils can reach. The question is how far you will let it go.

Once, during an exceptionally idle holiday in the Loire Valley, we hauled ourselves to Château de la Bussière, less for the Museum of Fishing, or even its medieval games, than for something to do. It was a hot hot day and nowhere would serve these scrappy late English people lunch. Disgruntled, we sat above the fragrant moat, eating one of those unsatisfactory picnics which so often feature in foreign travels: miscellaneous cheesy pastries, a piece of cheese, a white baguette and slices of cold pizza, each with its token circle of green olive. Then, because we had paid, we made a cursory tour of the grounds and there we came upon a spectacular potager: head-high blackcurrants like strings of dusty beads, wedding bouquets of artichokes and, best of all, a cucurbit walkway, a long green cave from whose ancestral ironmongery immense squashes and miniature pumpkins dangled like jewels. I shall not rest until I have one of my own and, thanks to 'Tromboncino', it may yet happen.

I don't have the metalwork, nor the soil in which to insert it. However, I have ingenuity. This year I trained my strongest climber by tying a bamboo cane to the viburnum and, with creative knot work, formed a home-made viney archway which did seem to tempt visitors to venture more deeply into the jungle, and not simply because I was prodding them from behind while emitting encouraging cries. If they were clunked on the head by a dangling toddler-sized cucurbit, they could count themselves blessed.

For, if one has been reasonably lucky with male flowers, the 'Tromboncino' is outrageously prolific. Its mighty fruits and gorgeous golden trumpets will keep appearing for months. Their skin is stronger, more apple than courgette, so they don't develop little runnels and age-spots of mould. The firm flesh remains, well, turgid, for days and days and days like its cousin, the butternut squash. You can add it to everything, but don't think of it as serviceable; it's much too entertaining for that. Add it to onion, garlic and fresh tomatoes, perhaps a bit of thyme, and cook it until the edges soften; add a little lemon zest and basil, of any variety. Delicious, practical and now not remotely phallic, more's the pity.

SISYPHUS

A sane person, and I must know some, would be sitting in a chair on this golden summer evening, drinking cold white wine and listening to the furry grumble of bees and birds and hoverflies and distant double-deckers. I've been out with the hose already, picked purple beans and redcurrants, fistfuls of mixed basil, two mugs-full of tomatoes, green, yellow and a strange boiled-chestnut purple-brown, whose long-lost labels could have told me so much. Now there is nothing to do but sit.

So why can't I?

These cosmos don't need cutting. I seem to have sown a horrible variety: ruffled white petals rimed with dark pink, like an Eighties interpretation of sexy underwear. Better to leave them for the pollinators; besides, unlike those cut-flower-patch pros, their bountiful armfuls of sweet peas and love-in-a-mist never quite hiding their smug smiles, I rarely produce enough to arrange in an eggcup, let alone a surprisingly expensive posy vase. These crazed planetary heads of calendula could be left to themselves; so many will have self-seeded already that, where once was a garden, next year will be a thicket of pot marigolds. It's too hot to plant the seedlings which cower, victims of overenthusiastic planting, under the bench; far too hot to consider pruning, dead-heading, let alone digging. What else is there to do?

Nothing. Go and sit down.

So why, in the name of heaven, can't I sit still?

Dorothy Parker famously said of the Yale Prom, 'If all the girls attending it were laid end to end, I wouldn't be in the least surprised.' For some reason I often think of that as I potter about in this little mess, checking my basil for miniature snails, hand-delivering worm casts to my strawberries. If the hours I spent here were laid end to end, think of the bestselling novels I could have written instead. I could have learned coding. I might even have learned to relax.

Now we're being unrealistic. I'm bored at the mere idea. While you sit here gazing into space, why don't I deal with that bit of ivy and, if you could pass me the loppers, I'll try to reach that snail, and while we're here I should check the gooseberry for sawfly, yes, every leaf, it won't take long, I gave them a good inspection this morning, oh and look, hundreds of fallen abutilon flowers in the containers, just like yesterday; I'll pick them out but also move the containers, and give me a minute to sprinkle these last bits of wood ash under the raspberries, I know this throwing motion is imprecise but I can't reach that far across the bed, oh, and while I think of it, I wonder if the new sunfl–

See? Relaxing is not an option. Gardening, on any scale, is a full-time job. With all these demanding plants, I have no choice; I need to look after them. Or is the truth that I want to?

We all need something to love; even novelists know this. It's how we make difficult characters less loathsome. The exhausting, grubby, difficult work of caring for children and old people builds devotion; the same applies to tending spaniels, or motorbikes, or cyclamen. When we fritter away hours searching for pretty yellow butterfly eggs on brassicas, it doesn't feel like duty, but an act of love: a matter of life and death. Checking every leaf of 'Pentland Brig' kale is quite restful; the eggs, in neat LED-pixel rows, squash easily to a neon liquid trace, like a smudge of yellow highlighter. Those that escape spend their formative days as well-camouflaged tiny green wormlets, nibbling tiny bites from the underside of the leaf so that the outer membrane is merely freckled. Does it matter? We never eat these huge ragged umbrellas;

the children call even the tenderest cavolo nero leaflets 'stringy greens'. Besides, if kale is allowed to perennialise, its stalk growing long and woody, its flowering shoots broken off to produce dozens more, it looks spectacular, at a distance: almost too good to eat. The line between beautiful and past its best keeps blurring. I now have several chest-high monsters, somewhere in the hinterland between kale and sprouting broccoli which, like smelly old lurchers, I could not bear to lose. This is a worry. Have I taken my obsession with edibles so far that they are now ornamentals?

Sometimes I tell myself that the work is justified by flavour. We are constantly told that home-grown vegetables taste better than their hydroponically grown pesticide-weaned supermarket cousins. I have never grown a full-size carrot; my harvest – a few marble-sized 'Paris Market', 2-centimetre-long 'Purple Haze' like goblin fingers – is always being pulled up accidentally, then eaten at once, mud and all. Healthy, yes, but, compared to supermarket carrots, grown for uniformity and sweetness, fairly disgusting. Fresh peas, if one rears them in pots as I do, crop by the teaspoonful. What vegetable gardener wouldn't want to grow sweetcorn: plump cobs thrown from garden to boiling water in a novelty relay race, hot butter, typewriter-style nibbling competitions, unsurpassed deliciousness? Also, my family are great ones for popcorn; imagine if we were self-sufficient. I'd never have to buy Butterkist Sweet 'n' Salted again. But a decent-sized, nicely spaced block in the end bed would mean goodbye to the gooseberries, the whitecurrants, the euphorbia and hellebores and rhubarb and the dogwood I bought suspiciously cheaply last weekend. So, every year, I compromise with only three or four plants and produce perhaps one cob, the size of a lunch-box banana. So why do I go to all this trouble? If we add the glee of collecting, the unequivocal deliciousness of thyme and raspberries, the murky pleasures of showing off, the joy of muddiness, the satisfaction of production and the soothing power of solitude, is that explanation enough for all this toil? How about my immigrant insecurity, the deep-rooted belief that, if I can chit potatoes and save wild cabbage seed, my family may survive? I'll admit, too, that there may be an element of hoarding involved. By chucking my poorly grown produce into the compost, so that I can grow more, I'm not so very far from turning into one of those people who is eventually crushed by a landslide of stored newspapers and coffee stirrers.

Perhaps we're all deluding ourselves: outdoors does not necessarily mean healthy. Like our minds, our bodies continually betray us. All gardeners are scarred and stiffened; everything hurts. Charles Dudley Warner, the American garden writer largely famous for having been carried, in his coffin, by Mark Twain, wrote, 'What a man needs in gardening is a cast-iron back, with a hinge in it.' Gardening attracts more than its share of aphorisms, but this one is true; I yearn for that hinge, and also for the minor superpower of levitation, and arms and legs which can telescope like loppers, and tiny feet like chamois hooves. Garden magazines are stuffed with advertisements for copper bracelets and glucosamine supplements, featuring sexually fulfilled-looking pensioners with rectangular glasses and enormous white teeth. It's because of all that bending. Our joints are knackered; after only a few years of right-angled slug-hunting and leaf inspection, my vertebrae have given up entirely. Non-gardeners don't understand the constant peril we endure. But, no, it's fine, I'll manage. Please don't help. Someone has to do it.

THIRTY-THREE ALTERNATIVES
TO LETTUCE

I'm sitting at my desk, arguably writing but, in truth, admiring a salad. I just made it for lunch. When I say 'just', it took perhaps half an hour of delightful browsing; we shall overlook that. Non-cooks aren't convinced by interesting salads. It's too much like cooking itself: stressful, complicated. Why not go to the local greasy spoon for a toastie? Yet, if one is a gardener-cook, on however modest a scale, there is little in life to match peacefully eating a plate of food from the garden.

The cookery writer Richard Olney, who was born in Iowa and moved to Provence the moment he could, devoted three pages of the hilariously named *Simple French Food* to instructions for 'the imaginative and playful, self-renewing invention of a giant composed salad, never once repeated, its composition dictated by the materials at hand ... [including] the far from frivolous presence of flowers and a sufficient variety of green things ... a concentrated, pulsating landscape of garden essences'. Pat, I discovered early in our acquaintance, shared his views. It was in her garden, where clematis grew horizontally and wild garlic waved outside the kitchen window, that I discovered that the greatest salads don't need bacon or croutons, but simply a combination of leaves and shoots and flowers.

Today's lunch for one, therefore, consists of toast, a boiled egg and, piled high around it like a jade-and-rainbow cloud: cinnamon and Greek and purple-ruffled basil; golden marjoram; grey-pink sage flowers; four or five kinds of cherry tomato; torn leaves of kale (perennial, ornamental, bog-standard); garlic and normal chives; land and normal cress; three kinds of chicory, both leaf and azure petal; red-veined rocket and sorrel and mustard and beetroot and chard leaves; the sulphur-yellow flowers of brassicas gone to seed. There is, I notice, technically no lettuce. But there are spicy nasturtium leaves like lily pads and their glowing honey-pepper orange blossoms; as many purslane seedlings as I can spare (three); little tastes of thyme and savory and rather more of parsley and chervil and lashings of mint; tiny lemon verbena leaves, dangerously close to end-of-season toughness; broccoli shoots; calendula and sunflower petals and whole borage flowers, their bitter sepals removed so that only the pistil and petals, the hot clear blue of a summer sky, remain.

It helps to have a really good vinaigrette. Today it's just lemon juice but, when guests come to dinner, I add olive and walnut oil, mustard, salt, a little honey. However much time I've spent on the other courses, it's the salad of which I am most proud, most affronted when they don't comment. Philistines.

EARLY AUTUMN

'He did not perceive that the most successful growers proceeded on exactly opposite lines to himself, namely, in planting many trees of a few wisely selected Varieties, instead of one or two trees of as many Varieties as he could obtain or find room for. He had quite a museum of Pears, interesting but unprofitable, and could happily afford to indulge in the luxury.'

Obituary of R. D. Blackmore (died 1900), author of *Lorna Doone*, quoted by Brent Elliott in the *Garden*, October 1992

PLEASE DON'T EAT
THE FLOWERS

I don't want to be negative, but this is a catastrophe. There has been too much sun, and too much rain: too much weather in general. Also, too few pollinators; occasional hoverflies, the odd low-buzzing bee or funny-looking dusty moth, but not enough to make this garden a cornucopia. I am hoping that this is the climate's fault, because otherwise it's mine.

If I can't stop eating the flowers, I'll have to plant more. What else can be done? Bees avoid the lovingly handmade nesting-boxes of sticks and straws, like badly reviewed bed and breakfasts. The ladybird larvae I bought online decided that the aphids next door were greener. All that nourishing potash-rich borage slime meant to encourage fruit and flowers, and the teabag contents, and the used matches, seem to have produced a metre-long vine of succulent pelargonium foliage climbing right up into the bay tree, but not much else. If one discounts the leafy victims of slug teeth and vine-weevil mandibles, the yellowed garlic chives and dead flowers, wasn't the healthiest greenery on the tomato plants, now removed?

Hold on, a reasonable reader might say. Where are the mounds of summer berries and squeaky bundles of spring greens, the sorrel soup and poached apricots and weeping figs and early apples, the glowing jars of cherry jam, the pickled cucumber? You've wittered on about your apparently innumerable fruit bushes, the time you lavish on your salads instead of your family. Where is the colossal harvest for which you and, frankly, we have waited so patiently?

Let us now probe an uncomfortable truth: the unidentified rustle in the compost bin, the maggot in the apple. Come with me, past the thicket of bamboo canes and the red and white Arsenal scarf, one hundred per cent pure polyester, with which the abutilon is lashed to its home-made and laughably inadequate supports. Squeeze past the allegedly blight-resistant tomato 'Lizzano', planted at the last minute in a bean pot when, after one too many damp days, I felt the Fear; the increasingly bald cavolo nero; the recumbent borage; the drooping foxgloves and hollow sunflower stems left for hibernating solitary bees; the disappointingly short dahlia and calendula, calendula everywhere. Here, taste this whitecurrant. I'm sorry, that's the lot.

The awkward truth is this: two whitecurrants are never enough. My maximum blueberry production to date has been one small mug; blackberries have been excellent this year, two crumbles' worth, but the other berries are limited to a couple each on our muesli. It's hardly the Dorchester's pudding trolley. I'm still buying enough fruit weekly to feed a smallish elephant, bunches of parsley and most of our vegetables from my substantial friend Oggy at the Saturday market, who gives me weekly reports on his complex family, tales of Lincolnshire farm life and an occasional courtesy flirt. We may be self-sufficient in unusual salad and bay leaves but, after all this, is that enough?

I would love to claim that it is, but I am a terrible liar. In truth, the frustration can make me weep. After my year in the wilderness we had the Year of the Builder, when plaster dust and MDF fibres and picturesque wood shavings covered the garden like beige snow all spring, all summer. The caterpillars invited their friends; the sawflies, tiring of gooseberry leaves, explored new taste sensations. By the time the dust had washed away and my strength had returned, there wasn't much garden left. But, slowly, I sowed and planted and grew and, a couple of years later, on the gardening online forum to which I was by now secretly addicted, I posted this:

is anyone else feeling real gardening despair?

First some positive facts:
1. *I completely and passionately love gardening – so I've had loads of joy and relaxation and interest this year, which isn't to be ignored.*
2. *determined to have realistic expectations about how much I can produce from my tiny plot/pots.*
3. *terrible rainy rainy weather.*
4. *raspberries, sorrel, kale doing brilliantly.*

OK. BUT … here are my results to date (and don't laugh at me) (much):
1. *tomatoes struck down with blight – a few handfuls edible, most probably won't ripen in time, and the rest made into chutney which am not sure I even like … pitiful I know.*

2. *maybe three handfuls of blueberries, three of wild/alpine strawberries.*
2a. *two INDIVIDUAL (not handfuls of) normal strawberries. Eight indiv. black-currants, twelve goosegogs, five whitecurrants. Two wineberries. Two sticks of rhubarb, maybe four blackberries – that really is the lot.*
3. *not a single bloody apple.*
4. *two to three tiny courgettes per plant before pulled out due to rot.*
5. *reasonable but not huge amounts of rocket, chicory, but hardly any 'normal' lettuce.*
6. *two individual as yet unidentified huge squashes.*
7. *nothing from homegrown chillies and aubergines, three bought seedlings of chillies with three titches between them, nursery seedling of aubergine dead.*
8. *four slightly ropy cabbages.*
9. *about five handfuls of mixed beans so far.*
10. *oh yes and not forgetting about seven broad bean pods.*

WHAT IS THE POINT?
Yes, great joy in the doing, but misery in the reaping ... and b/c I have little space every tiny failure counts. Soft fruit particularly disappointing. Not a cheap business, either.

Have fed soil and plants, guarded against birds (netting), searched for slugs most nights (yes), reasonably sheltered and reasonable sun I think, tended the little blight-ers like my own flesh and blood. Am I just a rubbish gardener?

I know most of you are super experienced and will tell me to buck up. But it's just a wash-out and I'm feeling very sad.

And then, gentle reader, as I waited for responses, I burst into tears.

There are many expert gardeners on this forum, largely good-hearted, and thousands of beginners whose disasters do wonders for one's mood. It's the ideal community: birthday wishes for the sociable; company for the lonely; Slovakian recipes for the experimental; detailed advice about every subject, from the chemical composition of PVC sheeting to how to grow blueberries from the seed of supermarket fruits. Every question, however idiosyn-cratic, will be answered; old sheds and onion sets and corms are given free-ly. I am deeply attached to the first kind members I encountered; I could spend weeks discussing the ideal leaf-mould density and swapping ginger-rhizome-sprouting tips.

My cry for help was answered. Within minutes, some of my favourites had replied. Most were generous; no one openly mocked. Nevertheless, they clearly thought I was ridiculous; I could feel the internet clutching its sides as, behind their privacy settings, they sent each other messages about this gender-nonspecific pedantic fool.

'Don't worry,' several consoled me. 'The first year is never easy.'

I have photographs of my harvests at that time, simultaneously beautiful and absurd: ten red and orange and golden tomatoes and a dozen green ones lying hopefully near a banana in order to ripen: purple and yellow and mottled and green beans, a couple of meals' worth; a football-sized mystery squash, ridged and golden as a fairy-tale carriage; a couple of 'Tromboncini', the light catching their curves and bulges. The yields are higher now, a little, but a new problem has occurred: I have developed a fear of picking.

Yes: at last, after a lifetime's effort, I have invented a brand-new neurosis for which there is, as yet, not even a name. Let's worry about that too while the puny fruits of my labours lie unharvested: nine morello cherries rotting on the tree; redcurrants I hope the birds will ignore. Grey fluffy strawberries hide among the red mizuna; they will have a satisfying end on the compost, the weird speeded-up life cycle for which I should probably seek help. The tiny pumpkins by the back door, which I had hoped would be sweltered into ripeness by puffs of humid steam from the boiler vent, add much-needed colour to the dwindling bean plants. I am saving the basil for something exciting. Will the slugs eat the single spinach plant before it runs to seed? I admire, I taste: no more.

Perhaps I'm simply paralysed by admiration: a whole bowlful of glossy blackberries or a single bunch of miniature grapes, plump with juice magically emanating from *this* sun, *this* soil. Come now. That isn't the whole truth, is it? The cherries wither and I'm still waiting for the optimum moment to present itself: the free afternoon when I will have time to make a magnificent wild-strawberry pavlova, the guest who will truly appreciate the few surviving leaves of golden purslane. I can't just squander it, when there is so little. I'm not a hoarder, I'm just ... cautious. So I wait, and wait, and the grapes rot.

NATURE'S BOUNTY

But no, it's fine. I'll struggle on. Owners of big gardens must have troubles of their own. When they write about scrubbing cherry juice off their flagstones, or suggest conscripting small children to de-strig blackcurrants, they mean well. I'm sure of it. We should pity them, really, for the exhaustion those rolling acres must bring. In any case, who needs orchards? Some of us, hungry and open-minded, are eyeing the glories of the hedgerow: free food. Foraging. The call of the wild.

Imagine a sniper in prime position, a jaguar about to drop down from its perch. Scientists monitoring shoppers in a National Trust tea room before a plant sale would doubtless find the same physiological responses as any hunter displays: stealth, ruthlessness, the fierce adrenal rush. But that is nothing compared to the complex yet shamefully basic sensations a forager feels in front of a hedgerow. Some addictions are difficult to diagnose. You may consider yourself non-addictive, even risk-adverse: too sensible for Vegas, too mature for cocaine. You may think that picking fruit in the open air is a healthful activity, to be encouraged. You would be wrong. Other than a helpless devotion to buying second-hand books, I have managed to resist the dangerous compulsions which affect my peers: fags, Prosecco, Earl Grey, running. Yet show me a puddle of fallen wilding apples beside a traffic jam on the A502 and I'll start exhibiting the classic symptoms of addiction: secretiveness, impulsiveness, irritability and an overwhelming craving to get my fix, at any cost.

It is the season of excuses. Is there a prolific bramble in the hedge on the longer route home from the shops? Let's take it; I need to, er, post a letter. Is there really an *Amelanchier lamarckii* in that neglected front garden, its ripe Juneberries ignored by passers-by? Don't worry, no one will notice my carrier bag. I could be climbing on this wall for a perfectly sensible reason.

There are philosophical issues; I am ready to discuss them, at length. Just how wild are those Oregon grapes if they're poking through the Pay and Display railings? That salad may contain dandelion but, if it's growing in a neighbour's breeze-block wall, is it truly wild? The intersection of town gardening and a passion for food is foraging of the most hideously bastardised kind. The eglantine rosehips grew plump on exhaust fumes and dog urine; the lime leaves whose glutinous crunch I relish in spring, and whose honeyed flowers are dried and kept in jars in French holiday homes for the English to ignore, are rank with petrochemicals. As I pick nettle tops I think of coast- and country-dwellers, feeding their young with wholesome greenery grown in real fresh air, and feel violent envy. West Yorkshire; Dartmoor; the Highlands; I should be anywhere but here.

I would love to claim to be a gardening renegade, a hedgerow pirate, but the truth is less swaggering. I lack courage. In a local front garden stands a resplendent crab apple, a 'Golden Hornet' or possibly 'Comtesse de Paris'. Every autumn its fruits ripen to a glowing, come-hither gold before falling, unloved, all over the carefully mown grass. The selfish fools know not the jewels that are theirs. So, do I, remembering every instruction in my *Junior Book of Spycraft*, observe the house carefully for signs of occupation, then steal noiselessly up the path and help myself? I do not. I prevaricate, agonise, then pass on.

Occasionally, greed does drive me to rashness. There is a grapevine on the next street, blocking the old wooden door at the end of its owner's garden. I would never, ever, hold possession of such a lovely brick wall with an old-fashioned garden door against them but how I covet those neglected grapes. They are everything a scoff-them-by-the-handful supermarket grape is not: thick-skinned, pippy, their bunches scrappy and sparse, like little bags sharply rich with juice. These grapes require one's attention. I keep picking samples for my family, which I then eat on the way home. But, for the nervous, stealing even underappreciated fruit is stressful. Most of the bunches hang above head height. A braver woman would bring a kitchen chair, even a stepladder; heart in mouth, I merely lurk on the corner, waiting for passers-by to pass by and yearning for a telescopic picking device.

Is this foraging or common theft? Some autumn fruits are more relaxing: the brambles on the heath, which vary so wildly from year to year in terms of location, and timing, and edibility, that I very rarely have competition. Who would fight for these few gritty berries, their drupes malformed or barely ripe, when one compares them to the plumptious glistening six-grammers of childhood? We all remember a place where the pickings were better; mine is the lanes down to the seaside in East Cork, where we spent summers arguing and weeping but, oh, the sun-warmed ozone-salty fruit.

Adulthood is a time of compromise; even cities contain interesting treasures, if one is desperate. My foraging passion unfortunately now extends to firewood: garage logs are expensive, so I drag home fallen branches like a disinhibited terrier, pretending not to notice the expressions on the faces of bystanders. Owners of reasonably sized gardens: next time you grab a handful of dead twigs for kindling, spare a thought for those who have to pluck them, one by one, from between park railings. I hoard tree bark for a clearly insane project involving drainpipes; store conkers among my jumpers because Italians say they repel moths – although not, apparently, English moths. And yesterday, passing a tree surgeon's van heaped with bay leaves, that rich sappy reek like roasting meat, our conversation about tree rings led, inevitably, to my attempting to carry home a barely liftable slice of trunk, damply pinkish-yellow as cake: too big to burn, too small to make a magical woodland table. 'Bays are beasts,' he said. 'Never plant one in open ground,' and I nodded wisely, trying to look like someone who hasn't done just that.

Let's not pretend it's a healthy outdoor hobby, this compulsion to lay in stocks for when the bad times come. I descend from a short line of terrified immigrants; this does not lead to security. I look at weeds and think: that's sheep sorrel, which we could eat at a push. Aren't roots supposed to be more nutritious? Better brush up on those. We could cultivate chickweed and fat hen and live on that, couldn't we? If it became . . . necessary?

As far as neurotic afflictions go, foraging is fun. At least, for the forager. Walking with me is like having an ill-trained toddler, particularly in autumn. Or spring. As I zoom off for a taste of fiery wall rocket, my poor children say patiently, 'Are you sure you should be eating that?' Gently, they refuse my offerings; I should feel grateful that they acknowledge me at all. If they lose me, they know I'll eventually reappear, glowing-cheeked and triumphant, pockets filled with sweet chestnuts of a particularly fat and satisfying variety. I have been grubbing about at the feet of passers-by, which I omit from the exciting account of my adventures.

'The great thing about growing older,' I tell them, twiggy-haired, encrusted with mud, 'is not caring what others think' and they look sadly at me.

'Yes,' they say. 'We know.'

TELL NO ONE

But the greatest thrill by far is gathering damsons.

Gardeners are generous. Like Labradors with muddy tennis balls, we long to share. One minute we're in a bus queue, the next we're discussing vermiculite or recommending raspberries: 'Honestly, trust me. "Joan J" is the answer, forget "Autumn Treasure". I got three canes in a special offer, though I didn't really need ... look, give me your address and I'll post you one.'

Even better is sharing with friends. At long last I have found a horticultural ally: Gabrielle next door, a glamorous costume designer who, when released from the demands of opera singers' embonpoints, tends a garden which is, unfairly, even smaller than mine. Gabrielle's presents so far have included: a magenta lychnis; cucamelon and basil seedlings; countless dried chillies; a cutting from her mother's arum lily; a bountifully flowering common sage; rare white beans and a French recipe for slug-repelling garlic spray. Over the garden wall, concealed from each other by branches and bamboos and, charmingly, the sticky papers I hang to keep my compost flies from her breakfasts, we discuss splitting pitifully modest brassica orders. If I were down to my last nematode family I would give it to her, and I know she would do the same. But will I ever tell her where I pick damsons?

Over my dead body.

There is no love great enough to share this secret. In the country, even the suburbs, damsons are quite common. I once came across a groaningly laden tree on the way to a school open day and, forcing my daughter to consume her sandwiches on the spot, filled her lunch box and pockets and my bag and hers. However, this is London, and wild plums aren't exactly rolling in the gutters of Baker Street. I am not too proud to pay £3 for a punnet, but there is nothing to compare to the inky sweetness of a real live captured damson, in the wild.

So nobody can know of my secret venue; the thought of meeting, even alerting, a fellow-forager makes me feel quite frantic. The question is: will there be any treasure to find?

This is my fourth season of picking. By now, I am quite professional: dark clothing to avoid attracting notice; hair tied back to prevent entrapment; shoulder bag; open plastic tubs; cover story. Of course I have a cover story. Nobody can be trusted. If anyone ever discovered this amazing secret, wild plums growing in central London, my vengeance would be swift and bloody.

My undisclosed location is not pretty. It is tight with twisted roots and untrammelled growth, as ragged with plastic bags as a crime scene. As I push inside, I rehearse lies: I'm looking for a dog. I've spotted – quick, what's a rare bird? A yellowhammer, or have I made those up? Would a squirrel do? The light is dim; I am hemmed in on all sides by scruffy hedgerow but no damson shall escape me. Thanks to a lifetime of minor fossiling, and my torch-lit pest-hunts, I can spot little blue wild plums cowering in the deepest foliage. I have set an alarm for three quarters of an hour. There is no time to waste. Damson-picking day always clashes with some minor irritant, like earning a living or feeding my family. But, for this short interval, with the scent of the hunt in the air and waterproof receptacles at my command, I am free, weightless, truly happy. I move deeper into the thicket. It is a magic wardrobe and I am already lost.

This never lasts for long. In the depths, disappointment waits. The ground is too choked for the spotting of windfalls, the trees are suffocating in the grip of hawthorn and blackthorn and ivy and hold their crops high on half-dead branches, too fragile to pull without raking off the ripe fruit. I have to freeze every time a runner passes; a rare exploring child happens upon me and I smile, as reassuringly as a woman can when caught in a spinney with purple-stained carrier bags, dramatically scratched and grinning like a fool. After only a couple of minutes my alarm sounds but I'm scratched and entangled, with barely a handful to show. I've got my eye in now, I think proudly, as if demonstrating my luge technique before the Winter Olympics selectors.

Yet my spirits are sinking. This time last year the fruits were green marbles; now they are scarce, and the remainders seem overripe. Have I missed the moment? Has someone beaten me to it?

The mere words fill my heart with ice. Guidelines exist for foragers. One must never, ever, take plants or bulbs of wild flowers, which is fine: you can keep your bee orchids. Gathering fruit, though, is governed more by etiquette. Don't take them all. Share nicely. Obviously *I* would if I had the chance (no I wouldn't), but someone has obviously been rather less well behaved. Sheepish and sad, I'm edging back out of the hedgerow now, my damson lust unslaked. There is no alternative but to go round to the public side of the hedge.

This is extremely stressful. Like any deviant forced to get their kicks in public, I fear exposure, but my need is stronger. Now anyone could see me, leaf-strewn, tangle-haired, peering into the shadows; worse, they might expect me to share. I can definitely see some and now my excitement alternates with fevered invention: should I say I thought they were sloes? Bullaces, except that I don't know how to pronounce them, and aren't they really just rounder damsons, so just as covetable? There are still not enough to satisfy me. I am reduced to picking up windfalls, risking earwigs, decay, public humiliation because this is my annual harvest. I can't go home with bags this light. A few are ripe enough to eat from the tree; I pocket the stones to plant in the spring, convincing myself that although all domestic fruit trees have been grafted on to rootstocks, a wild and spindly damson might flourish without one (I look it up at home; it won't). And already I'm worrying about the ethics of home-grown wild fruit: would I enjoy the bounty or secretly hate myself for taking the easy way out, like playing cowboy at a dude ranch where the horses are discreetly broken in? Is a damson from a garden much more than a runty plum?

LET'S ALL STOP BOTHERING
WITH ANGELICA

It is gritty. It is bland. If you add it to Madeira cakes for an old-fashioned thrill, it will do nothing for you. Even the real stuff, which allegedly has a faint whiff of muscatel, is the least multi-purpose ingredient ever invented. Jekka McVicar, herb expert, who has boiled evening primrose roots (parsnipy) and deep-fried meadowsweet (nasty), claims that one can make jam out of it, tasting slightly of gin, but why not just add gin to a more serious jam? It's a good-looking plant, but no more so than the huge ostrich feathers of artichokes and lovage. It is also invasive, can paralyse the nervous system and is feared by witches. Yet I and, presumably, others with my affliction, have devoted minutes of my life to wondering whether to grow it, in order to perform the laborious process of candying it, which includes thrice-boiling, peeling, oven-drying and leaving it for two days in a cool place, covered in sugar syrup, which I'd quite like to have done to me, but not to do. Since we're here, I should perhaps also mention the lustful glances I send my neighbour's sumac tree, whose rusty spikes, like the antlers of an ailing moose, can be cleaned and dried and ground. By this stage even Jekka has lost interest. Then there are the olives which, two years ago, ripened beautifully on my little tree from violet to bruise to almost black. No source could agree on what to do next; I brined and refreshed them daily for weeks until they looked so repulsive that I had to throw them out, yet there I was, the following Boxing Day, so excited to realise that *green* olives might be preservable that I sneaked out barefoot in the dark to pick them, by touch.

The truth is never pretty. Fellow Preservers Anonymous members, I can reveal that home-made mint syrup is both useless and disgusting. Merely reading the words 'spruce oil' in a restaurant review has given me yearnings I cannot control. I developed such a passionate need to try the young fronds of a fiddlehead fern that, when I read in Alan Davidson's *The Oxford Companion To Food*, one of my favourite bath-time companions, that it may be carcinogenic I felt the deep relief of an addict briefly saved from total degradation.

It's all Laura Ingalls Wilder's fault. She has a great deal to answer for already: generations of girls now believe that, because their waists are bigger than Ma's, they will never marry a man like Pa, or ride in a covered wagon to a prairie. However, her most pernicious influence is in the field of preserving. Even before I had bought *The Little House Cookbook* for its Spit-Roasted Wild Duck and Fried Apples 'n' Onions, the nine books about the Ingallses had seduced me. Like countless English children I longed, and still long, for salt-churned ice-cream; for sun-dried huckleberries and rainwater vinegar and cucumber pickles. What escaped me was the small matter of necessity: when in *Farmer Boy* Laura wrote, 'There was no rest and no play for anyone now. They all worked from candle-light to candle-light. Mother and the girls ... were drying corn and apples, and making preserves', it wasn't because Ma and Grace and Laura needed a bonding activity and couldn't agree on a box set, but a response to seasonal plenty and year-round want.

Yet there are times when even I am faced with green tomatoes, a plethora of blackberries, more chillies than I can use. Surely then preserving is valid, even necessary? And, conversely, isn't pickling and bottling and drying a time-honoured and therefore perfectly valid leisure activity?

Up to a point, just as wine with dinner is reasonable but wine *for* dinner is not, I have not yet stooped to buying new jamjars, preferring instead to surprise my family with avalanches when they open kitchen cupboards, but the passata mills and bags of corks in foreign supermarkets stop me in my tracks with naked desire. Online shopping is risky for any obsessive; a glancing reference to an out-of-print rye-bread recipe and I, who begrudge £1.50 for an espresso, find myself tracking rare hardbacks in the dead of night. Tired and over-caffeinated, one can convince oneself that buying a dehydrator for one's immense wild strawberry harvest would be a reasonable, even frugal, investment. At the time of writing, I have so far managed not to buy a grain grinder, because this household essential is available only in solid beech and ceramic, for £335, postage not included, but my desire to eat bread made from wheat I have grown myself – I'd give up a square foot of garden for it, maybe even two – is unabated.

There is no rest. Like an alcoholic searching for lighter fluid I'm past caring. I have found the only local supplier of citric acid, laboriously gathered elderflowers in the early morning (retaining the pollen but removing insect bodies) in order to make syrup which I then have no room to store. I can't resist picking medlars, fondling their russet rough skin and admiring their shape, the top pointed as an acorn, splayed open at the base like a fat brown rosehip, but have you ever tried to persuade family members to eat rotten fruit? I also produce countless revolting banana chutneys and pippy jams. I invented Heath Jelly, which uses not only all the disappointing hedgerow fruits, hips and haws and elderberries I can find in the nearby thickets, but also any Japanese quinces, crab apples and sloes I can pinch on the way home. It's perfectly pleasant, a gently aromatic soft-pink jelly which I find almost unbearable to part with, giving its lucky recipients such complex and passionate explanations of its birth that they look buffeted, like victims of mugging in reverse.

Yet, when February comes and we can spend a tenner on a handful of Seville oranges, who has the strength of mind not to make marmalade? These days I save my energies for Nigel Slater's Lime and Lime Leaf and try not to imagine Ma Ingalls's face if she could see the bill for the unwaxed limes, the Fairtrade sugar, the oddly short-lived kaffir lime tree I bought as a nest-egg.

I am prey to every false economy you can imagine. Having fallen under the fatal spell of Patience Gray's *Honey from a Weed*, on every foreign holiday I find myself scrabbling up rocky paths in search of wild juniper, while my children weep about scorpions and cry, 'But we can buy it in the shop!' Once home, I start yearning for a dry wall on which to grow a caper plant, *Capparis spinosa*; I bought a stunted barberry on special offer in case it happened to be the variety with delicious lemony berries. I live ten minutes from a Middle Eastern shop where they sell them, cleaned and dried, for a pound a packet. Even if the tree had fruited, and its fruits had been edible, how could this ever have been a good idea?

With ingenuity, there are infinite chances to waste money. Imagine making one's own Ribena, or rosehip tea, or oatmeal. Think of all those healthy Scandinavians, reared on sea-buckthorn jam. I may need to harvest pine nuts. There may be little point in pickling nasturtium buds but at least I know when to pick them, should it come to that. I'm being powerfully drawn to burdock. Help me, someone. It's getting bad.

For the suggestible and greedy, cookery books are a source of constant peril. We are at the mercy of the whims of their writers; one may have had no previous desire to make watermelon-rind jam or blueberry butter but, once it has been mentioned, how can one resist? I hate sauerkraut but I long to ferment; although I am not a nineteenth-century German student and dislike rum, I am currently racked with desire for a hideous earthenware pot, decorated with faux-naïf fruit depictions, for the making of *Rumtopf*. It is unfortunate that the more traditional preserving handbooks have been nudged aside by a new world of exciting picklings and saltings: Siberian spiced crab apples, carrot kimchi, Greek spoon sweets, Turkish dried vegetables, white miso. Thanks to pioneers such as Claudia Roden and Nigella Lawson, our store cupboards are now dangerously full of things we might actually want to eat.

This doesn't mean we're saving money. Because I trust the garden writer Alys Fowler, I tried fruit leathers. She was right; they are fabulous, addictively sharp concentrations of fruitiness in rollable form but, once one has mixed one's berries with organic Bramleys and ladles of honey, laboriously puréed them through an insufficiently wide-meshed sieve and dried them in a low oven for a good twenty-four hours, they are not an economy food. If I'm honest, they brought me close to ruin.

Reader, learn from the foolishness of others. Listen to my sorry tale. One of my favourite activities is swearing. It is satisfying, startling, addictive and does not give one cancer. However, in certain situations the swearing increases. I was sieving blackberry-pulp when my godmother dropped by. Boiling fruit goo and bad words were filling the air. My godmother is a practical woman and so, when my children complained about their stevedore mother, she decided to help them. She proposed a swearing box, 'proceeds to charity' and here was the kicker: the fine would double every week.

I was distracted. I forgot to put an upper limit on the doubling. A pound a swear-word became two, then four and, before I knew it, I had contributed £294 to the Royal Society for the Protection of Birds, for the simple honest pleasure of saying 'bugger'.

DOWN WITH NATURE

Like most omnivores and gardeners, my prejudices are random and unjustifiable. I do know that one ought to care about birds. Every gardening magazine insists upon the charms of thrushes and house sparrows. I have a friend who spends holidays chasing black woodpeckers in the Ukraine. However, although owls do interesting things with their necks and in Bloomsbury shopping centre I once enjoyed meeting a pigeon-scaring hawk, with bright orange talons and an air of psychopathic insouciance, I confess that I prefer plants.

Tadpoles are sweet but frogs are alarming. Newts are permanently tainted by Ken Livingstone. I won't eat Bambis or hares but devour adorable lambkins. I ignore childish pleas to rig up a bird feeder, lest its constant light rain of delicious rodent snacks attracts rats, yet pretend not to have noticed the grey mice in the compost bin which, when caught by brave Hercules, make me incoherent with panicky revulsion. Sometimes he drops them lovingly on the duvet; if he isn't praised he'll raise his game and bring in larger items, but it's difficult to bellow 'Good cat' convincingly as one barricades oneself in a child's bedroom, jittery with sleep deprivation and Blitz spirit.

Are vegetarians as violent? And, if we kill molluscs, why not woodlice, or kittens?

I confided my longing for a resident hedgehog to my cousin Maurice, an expert naturalist who keeps bees in Highgate Cemetery.

'You'll never have one,' he said, casually. 'They're on their way to extinction' and, with that, a childhood dream died.

This year, every scheme to lure pest predators has failed. I ordered hoverfly larvae; they didn't flourish. I stole individual adults from a local lime tree but they disappeared. My simple request to a friend for the hibernating ladybirds in his curtains was rebuffed: some nonsense about stepladders and stairwells. Garden magazines are full of aquatic pest-eating ideas: ducks for wireworms, toads for aphids, but some of us don't have space for a puddle, let alone a pond.

But today, 21 October, as I sadly prodded a waterlogged squash flower, a bumblebee the size of a greengage rumbled right past my ear: so furry, so fatly striped that it seemed impolite not to offer it my thumb to perch on; maybe even a sandwich. I wanted to stroke it, to sing to it. Does it have a family? And if so, would it seem creepy if I offered them all a bedroom? Just until next spring?

MID AUTUMN

'The gardener's autumn begins in March,
with the first faded snowdrop.'

Karel Čapek, *The Gardener's Year*

IT'S THE MOST WONDERFUL
TIME OF THE YEAR

Poor flower-gardeners. For fans of lupins and lobelias, it is a time of sorrow. Everything is bending, browning, suffering from too little weather or too much, submitting to the fate which awaits us all: defoliation, discoloration, death.

Never mind them. For the rest of us, meandering round our gardens with heads full of half-remembered odes and pockets full of misplaced labels, joy awaits. Our sunflower heads glisten invitingly; the last blackcurrants are tensely ripe; moggies lie louchely on the warm bricks with expressions of dusty hauteur. There is sun, in manageable quantities: bright rather than hot, infinitely cheering, it is impossible not to rush into the garden the moment it emerges, at half-minute intervals. And there is rain.

Rain is a great divider. Children barely notice it; teenagers consider it, like everything else, all about themselves, writing sad poems about drizzle, taking off their shoes to frolic self-consciously in thunderstorms. Then, as adulthood beckons, rain becomes a hindrance. Will anyone come to our flat-warming barbecue? How will my grey suede ankle boots survive the journey to work? It cramps our style; that, we are pretty confident, is all there is to say about rain.

But no: a more advanced stage is still to come. When you look outside at a downpour, do you think, 'Oh hooray – good for the garden'? Do you run to gather rusty old containers and position them for optimal water-harvesting? Do you, when you notice that the downpour has passed quickly, feel a sense of disappointment? Then you are a gardener: the highest point to which humankind has evolved.

Yet other, more mature gardeners take this further. They can make comparisons: 'Remember how dry last September was?' they say. 'And 2006; how many inches of rain was it on that Thursday: three? Two?' Politely I nod; I have no idea. Where do they file this information? I'm not sure I believe it. Just as 'the size of Wales' has become a universal unit of measurement, every single month we are told it is the hottest, or wettest, 'since records began'. I have ceased to listen. I live in the moment. Is it raining? No?

Never mind. I'll clear the outside table, laboriously, so we can have lunch in the fresh air; that will make it start.

QUINCES: A LOVE STORY

Only a gardener would appreciate my garden now. The bean leaves have turned yellow and begun to fall; most of the salad has bolted and the rest is filigreed by tiny brown slugs barely bigger than a semi-colon. The beds are being blanketed by expiring borage, immortal evergreen leaves, pock-marked kale and the damp sports socks which fall from my neighbour's roof-terrace railing like spring rain. The best self-seeders this year have proved to be the greenish-black ivy berries which lurk like little viruses, waiting for their chance to colonise. And, saddest of all, my poor bald tomato plants, supported by increasingly elaborate slings and tourniquets, may turn their faces hungrily to the last rays of sun but the last fruits have missed their chance.

Every gardening article witters on about the joy of a sun-warmed tomato. I wish they would shut up. Blight is coming, great waves of *Phytophthora infestans* rumbling in on the wind, splodging the haulms with peppery brown and turning the fruit from promising to puckered and ashy overnight. I check constantly for encouraging signs (Black Cherry go greyish; the Tigers develop paler stripes) and then they're ripped off the vine and hustled into the kitchen, where they quietly subside, leaving their dried calyxes curled at the bottom of the bowl like joke-shop spiders.

It is the end of fig season. This year's harvest was virtually Calabrian: of the five, two fell off and discreetly rotted before I could make myself pick them; the others hang there still, lightly browning in the remaining sun. I offer one to the children, excited and rather moved, but the fruit flies are more interested. It's the same when I pick blackberries; they lie forgotten unless I roam the kitchen, popping berries into the children's mouths like a mother bird. Eventually I slice off the soggy top layer and eat it in two gulps: sweet, fragrant, with a hint of sharpness but a fig, an ordinary fig, nothing more.

Bounty comes from another source. Our car usually reeks of fermenting orange peel, dried wet-wipes, anti-freeze and insoles but, for the past week, it has been scented like a Tudor pudding. I want to move in, keep inhaling that scent of roses, cloves, lemon. If I never open a window, how long can the quince-smell last?

This year has been famously Good for Fruit, which is just an excuse for proper gardeners to flaunt their Pippins. However, for the first time my dwarf quince made the difficult transition from those pretty saucer-shaped blossoms to tiny fruit. They looked unlikely to succeed: green overlaid with khaki felt, no bigger than a broad bean. But, slowly, with plenty of rainwater, a mulch of fir needles, and daily visits, like a grandparent who definitely knows best, I watched the fruits swell and go on swelling, until I no longer fretted about size and merely removed any leaves which dared to block the sunlight. Then, overnight, one fruit acquired a mystery blemish: a clear thumb-mark in its fuzzy coating. Could this mean a member of my family had approached one, touched it; that someone was, unprecedentedly … interested? Unlikely; as all gardeners know, nobody cares as much as we do. I kept my excitement to myself. A few days later I found the quince on the ground, lightly slug-marked. It sits before me on the kitchen table, too precious to cook, hard as potatoes.

I have always wanted quinces. One September, as I gorged myself on free samples at the Union Square Farmers' Market in Manhattan, in my cidery-arugula-baked-ham-maple-syrup daze I spotted a hand-written sign:

Quintz, $2.99

Quinces play it cool. They are the opposite of a wanton supermarket strawberry: exotic, complex and, like most inappropriate love objects, horribly elusive. If one is lucky enough to live near one of those corner shops with mysterious year-round supplies, for a pound one can buy an almost-quince: freakishly unblemished, barely fragrant. This is how my grandmother bought them before, in her windowless galley kitchen, peeling and slicing them, probably with a sabre, then poaching them with vanilla until they were soft and silkily rosy and her flat smelled like Samarkand. We could each have a quarter, maybe two; there is no such thing as too much quince. At least, so I thought.

'Come and look at this,' said Tim.

Tim is my jam husband; the only person I know who cares as much about the niceties of chutney, about Korean minimarkets and fern nurseries and flour strength as I do. However, our bond may not survive what happened last week, in his garden. He led me down to the end of the long lawn (something else to hold against them) and there, at the end, was the quince tree. I'd visited it before, paid homage but this year it was illuminated, every twig weighted with glowing golden fruit, like light bulbs among the dusky leaves.

I gasped.

Poor innocent man. 'Help yourse—' he began as, like an unleashed greyhound, I shot inside its dim canopy. There, with fat ripe fruit suspended on every side, sweet-smelling, with a prickle of alcohol, a whiff of *eau de vie*, it felt as if I was deep in its quincey heart. For a townie, nothing can match the heady thrill of untrammelled fruit-picking, of knowing that for every one we choose we have the luxury of plenty more: so many more than we could possibly need. I couldn't stop grinning. First I picked from below, then on tiptoe from the wall beside it and, if Tim was demurring as I stripped his tree, I sadly couldn't hear him. I'd probably have brained him if he'd come inside.

Children visited, to laugh; I was too busy pillaging to speak. I could have picked double, triple, but restrained myself from filling a third carrier bag. Never mind our close family friendship; I need to get at that tree next year.

First I admired my quinces, for several days: the biggest already so richly ripe, the smaller fruit still tinged with green at the lobed flower end, or lopsided, dimpled with odd imperfections or thicker fuzz. I closed my mind to the thought of their sisters, still unpicked.

'Isn't the smell fantastic?' I demanded of everyone who came into the kitchen, even if they'd just gone out for milk.

'Shouldn't you cook them?'

'They'll be fine,' I insisted. This was a lie. Paralysed by indecision, I was beginning to panic: cake? Jam? Compote? Membrillo?

Tim would know about membrillo. 'Don't even try,' he said. 'Waste of a week.'

So I stewed some with apples, poached three with saffron, and then, despite lacking most of the vital equipment, I made jars of pointless jelly.

'Look at my lovely quinces!' I cried to every visitor. Even I could hear the panic in my voice. What next? Spoon sweets? Pickles? Some kind of ketchup? Then I remembered about fruit leathers.

It was a terrible idea. As everyone knows, cut quinces brown; peeling and quartering and coring and trimming and slicing and cooking and mashing maybe fifteen of them at top speed, together with the wrinkling and pippy Japanese quinces I had pinched a fortnight before from a front garden, cost me several hours and part of a finger, which bled prettily on the quince flesh. At last, the sweetened purée drying behind me in a barely warm oven, looking like vomit but smelling of heaven, I sit mistyping this love story, my index finger wrapped in several types of plaster, hitting *v*s and *n*s instead of *b*s.

It doesn't matter. At least the *q*s are safe: my love is secure. But, like a suitor, I am secretly fretting that I mis-chose it after all; I should have chopped and frozen them, or baked them in wine until they gave up their pink juices, or just gazed at them as they rotted in their bowl: a portrait of entropy.

[Author's Update: my hopes are shattered. I'd imagined the quince leathers as a sort of portable membrillo but, in my determination to keep the sugar low enough to taste the tartness, I compromised their lives. I have just checked the jar; the leathers have gone fluffy. Bloody Tim.]

WHAT IS THE POINT OF ROSES?

Roses are quinces' relatives: show-off cousins in tight dresses, dancing inappropriately with Grandpa at family weddings. Is this why the British love them so? Are they our only chance of self-expression?

Roses are essential to our native idea of a garden. They litter our myth and language, from William Blake's 'Oh Rose thou art sick' to the very idea of a desirable woman as an English rose, rosy-cheeked; we even fought a war entirely over the question of whether white or red roses are better (the answer is white, as any fool knows). But what about Homer's rosy-fingered dawn or Lynn Anderson singing '(I Never Promised You a) Rose Garden' or Edith Piaf's 'La Vie En Rose'? Or the Brothers Grimm or Hans Christian Andersen? How embarrassing. Maybe Britain doesn't have exclusive claim to *Rosa* after all.

Roses are the flowers to end all flowers, the ones we sing and paint and compare our beloveds to. They have something for everyone: scent for the hedonist, thorns for the tattooist, vigour for the impatient, variety for the collector, hips for the hungry. Tired women at traffic lights sell them by the lurid dozen. Eddy, the retired black-cab driver up the road, has a paved front garden with three violently pruned yellow roses, still proudly bearing their nursery label. My grandparents' ashes lie in a suburban secular crematorium with assorted clairvoyants, artists, town councillors, widows and rock stars, united by the horrible lollipop standards on their resting places. Who doesn't love a rose?

Well, me. So many crimes against decency are committed by rose-growers that boycotting the lot seems perfectly fair. How often do you bend to sniff a neighbour's roses, leprosy yellow or knicker pink, only to discover that they are entirely scentless? Roses frequently make scruffy plants, as prone to nasty-sounding plagues as the most unfortunate medieval peasant. Their catalogues read like dog pedigrees; they are frequently overbred and underwhelming, prissily miniature or oppressively rampant, with stupid names ('President Hoover', 'Scentimental', 'Dorothy Perkins', 'My Dad') and delusions of grandeur. Yes, of course an ivory 'Mme Alfred Carrière' dripping over an ancient Oxford limestone arch is beautiful. 'Mme Isaac Péreire' is glorious on French manoir walls, the luscious pink heads glowing kir-royale purple on late summer evenings as the courtyard fills with the scent of ripe Epoisses and infidelity. But few of us have mellow Cotswold stone to spare. I can overlook the burbling rills and stone walkways of Mirabel Osler because her *A Gentle Plea for Chaos* has brought me so much joy but, when she lets slip that she owns 'eighty or ninety' types of rose, my empathy falters.

Some people dream of rose gardens. I dream of abandoning the unfragrant and hard-pruned altogether. Bring on the nanny state; imagine if only those with space were licensed to grow roses – fat creamy 'Tranquillity' to press our faces into; the scented glories, 'Gertrude Jekyll' and 'Comte de Chambord', for orgies of inhalation – while the rest of us focused on the beauties within our reach: the brainy ridges of Savoy cabbage; the secret veins in gooseberries; the tiny snowball buds of cherry blossom; the fat ball of sharp sweetness held tightly inside an apple skin; or the miraculous, perfectly straight, smooth mystery of a really good garlic chive.

TREE ENVY

Picture two school friends: one, the owner of a fine legal mind, the other ... not. Both have a dream of owning a plum tree. The first knows exactly the one to choose: a 'Hauszwetsche', technically a sweet variety of damson, known in Britain as German prune, in France as *quetsche d'Alsace*, in Germany as *Zwetsche* and in the United States as Italian plum-prune. Its fruits are sharp-skinned and sweet-fleshed, firm, not juicy: the perfect variety for *pflaumenkuchen*, a German plum tart for which this friend has been famed since childhood. They are productive, self-fertile, pretty trees. She invests in a well-grown teenage specimen, has it professionally planted in her frankly colossal garden and today, as trees should be, it is symmetrical and thickly covered in bloomy purple plums.

Which tree will the other choose? Surely not this one, of a similar age but the victim of poor pruning, pot-grown for several years therefore expensive but spindly, beginning to stoop due to lack of staking, thin trunked? This tree is a Cambridge Gage; gages, unlike plums, need good soil and full sun and take several years to begin cropping. The tree endures a garden-centre sale but remains unbought. Then, at last, salvation. It is adopted, repotted, fed and fleeced and nurtured and, to date, has produced not a single plum.

This is why my friend is a successful lawyer with more fruit than she can cook, and I am a novelist.

Beware of pity, particularly when combined with an eye for a terrible bargain. Gardeners with room to spare must curse themselves when, soft-heartedly, they yield to a plant in need. The rest of us can get into serious trouble. There was only ever going to be one plum tree in this garden, and so many other better choices. Was it really wise to foster the last horrible yellow peony at the plant fair; the unwieldy *Elaeagnus* at a school fête; the sad crab apple; the pair of hibiscus left in bin bags outside a neighbouring house? Is this how one becomes a cat woman? Might it have been kinder to have left these unfortunates to better parents, who could have given them space to roam?

FALLING IN LOVE AGAIN

Do you suffer from garden envy? When you visit famous houses, do you struggle not to grab a wheelbarrow and race around the borders, laughing maniacally as you uproot rare astilboides and Chrysanthemum 'Emperor of China', before legging it to the exit?

Of course you do. All the best people are greedy. I'm just puzzled about why, covetous and plant-crazed as I am, I don't feel the same. Famous gardens are frustrating, not inspiring. I remember the bridge at Giverny and the topiaried Irish yews at Dartington but, unless thoroughly shredded, they wouldn't fit here. Even I know I don't have space for a Lost Gardens of Heligan gunnera. Yes, I love the murky uncompromising green of the Barbara Hepworth Sculpture Garden but, without her colossal bronze and stone sculptures, and a view over the rooftops of St Ives to the sea, wouldn't this yucca just be . . . a yucca? I wouldn't say no to the tower at Sissinghurst but settle for an eponymous verbena: a rich pink, trailing from nineteenth-century bronze urns near the entrance arch. Strangely it wasn't sold in the shop; I found it years later, in one of the rural garden centres which dot Britain, all bird seed and rat traps and under-the-counter ammunition. But my little verbena seemed less elegant in a window box near a catflap; I felt cheated, as if the Nicolsons were laughing at me through binoculars.

Yet, at Beth Chatto's nursery, I wanted everything. We had come to East Anglia to research my fifth novel but, once I realised how close we were to her famous gardens, of which I had read in her delicious *Garden Notebook* all that glorious Georgian brick, the smugglers' creeks and saltings became unendurable. Even the borage fields of Wilkin and Sons, the Tiptree jam company, were powerless to thrill. I had taken all the notes I needed: flatness, samphire, boats. Right, that's it. Shouldn't we head home, via Elmstead Market? Ideally, in the next five minutes?

I bet Mrs Chatto has binoculars, and so will definitely have spotted how one sensitive visitor was instinctively drawn to the handsome grey leaves and huge white rumpled petals of her Californian tree poppy, *Romneya coulteri*. Certainly, when she totted up the till receipts that night she must have been impressed by one particular customer: 'Ah, *Thymus neiceffii*! Good choice. And so few people appreciate the loveliness of an *Origanum* "Kent Beauty". *Fragaria vesca* "Golden Alexandra" *and* an *Agastache rugosa* "Golden Jubilee"? Well played, anonymous buyer. Well played.'

The point of the Beth Chatto gardens is not edibles; the thyme and oregano are only there because the bees love them so. Yet even my vegetable-fixated heart was won by the little patches of silver-leafed ground cover beneath mullein spikes, the lambent blue of Russian sage, the flowered mats of creeping catmints and grasses. I scribbled frantic notes in the margins of my entrance ticket:

Purp Emp sedum = maroon cauliflower – lovely
Verbena officinalis var. *grandiflora 'Bampton'* like mine but better;
~~Tru Tu~~ *Teucrium hircanicum* × *lucidrys* i.e. Caucasian germander, tiny shiny leaves.
CARDOON.

Then, as I turned a gravelly corner, bluebirds twittered around my head, the air seemed to sparkle as, in slow motion, my gaze fell upon an unassuming rosy flower.

Crazes are so irritating. For every early adopter, there are grumps like me who refuse to be told what to like. We'll wait until everyone else has entirely lost interest before, grudgingly, we'll take a look. And so, as a matter of cussed principle, I have never appreciated non-edible alliums. Their bulbs are expensive, their flowers are drab pink or lilac, and everyone has them. Then I saw *Allium sphaerocephalon*, and fell in love.

Allium sphaerocephalon lacks the pyrotechnic sparkle of its flashier cousins: *schubertii*, like something sent to a gardening magazine by a worried reader, or 'Hair', which could be one of the Muppets. It is modest, even sober: oval-headed as a plum, perhaps a little tufty at the top, a deep magenta like red clover, with a clover's greenish-white lower parts. Its stems are as spindly as certain grasses; in the Gravel Garden it grew in natural-looking clumps against a backdrop of *Festuca glauca*, bearded irises and agapanthus. I don't have an agapanthus; I don't even have any gravel. There is no obvious reason why I desired it so, although its loganberry-purple resembled the best felt-tip pen I ever had, free with a poster, 'Under the Sea', which I spent my thirteenth year colouring in while eating chocolate digestives. It was progress, I decided now, to admire a flower which couldn't be lunch. I must be becoming more sophisticated, at last.

Months later, when I got hold of the bulbs, I discovered that, as well as being known as 'drumstick allium', it is sometimes called 'round-headed leek' and is, allegedly, edible. I could pretend that I mind, that I was looking forward to having plants in my garden whose beauty alone excited me. It would be a lie. I can't wait to eat one; indeed, I just looked it up on the marvellous Thompson & Morgan online list of edible flowers and discovered, too, that tulip petals are perfectly fine in salads. This changes everything.

AMATEUR BURGLARY

Beth Chatto is a lucky woman. She is too old, too posh and too uninterested to be a celebrity; she can spend her days as the owner of a famous garden who writes wonderful books. Celebrity gardeners are a strange species: the aristocracy of entertainment. Their ways are not for the likes of us. Television cooks have to pretend to be normal people so we will believe we too can whip up tagliatelle and dim sum for close friends. Gardening celebrities are more open about what separates them from the mortals. The unattainability of their sit-on mowers, their shaded paths and grass mounds and wooden glades for quiet contemplation are the point; it makes them divine. We know that even if we queue to buy their books at gardening shows, all we can hope for is an idea: a bit of slate, a clump of *Stipa gigantea*. When they broadcast-sow a native meadow on virgin soil raked to an icing-sugar tilth, the result will be waving vistas of wood anemones and orchids. A pack of pound-shop Mixed Wildflower (Brights) chucked over the rubbly bit in the corner will have quite a different effect.

It can't be easy, being a famous gardener. The poor loves inhabit a fictional world, constantly smiling in their trademark outfits (avuncular crew-necks, autumnal hand-knit scarves, velvet Edwardiana) as they slice hostas into chunks with copper spades. We may have televised glimpses of their private terraces, buy 'their' seeds and secateurs like holy relics, yearn for cosy chats about *Rudbeckia* 'Marmalade' with lovely Carol Klein, but we know that we are but humble imitators, and they are our gods.

Famous gardens and public parks are another matter entirely. Most of us are too moral, or too afraid of prison, to nick entire plants. Seed heads, provided they are common and plentiful, are harder to resist. At this time of year, when the sun seems to be losing interest and the garden is beginning to decline, temptation waits.

I come from a line of thieves. When we cleared out the flat of my late grandmother, a woman so congenitally generous she distributed small presents wherever she went, we discovered a hoard of stolen ashtrays, restaurant crockery and hundreds of ballpoint pens, some still chained to their weighted pen-holder. My father, a law-abiding man, owns a surprising number of hotel dressing-gowns and once brazenly walked through Customs pretending not to be holding a child-sized coconut palm in a pot, which he had liberated from a roadside.

Like any robber's child, I have tried to escape the amorality to which I was heir, but I have failed. Whether I'm at a primary-school fête, assessing a straw bale as a possible mushroom-growing medium, or wondering if a municipal maple tree might slake my family's unquenchable syrup thirst, or debating whether those scaffolders would notice if I pinched a plank, just a small one, or eyeing up the wild strawberries planted outside the British Library, larceny is always on my mind. Whether I've bounded through the gates of a serious garden, like Waterperry in Oxfordshire or Ballymaloe House in Cork, or am merely passing a neighbour's front wall, I barely notice the pretty flowers. All I can see is common annual seeds.

Marigolds! Sweetpeas! Poppies, hollyhocks, love-in-a-mist, cornflowers, half-dried beans! In childhood I read far too many books which fuelled my gluttony: the Big Rock Candy Mountain where the chickens lay soft-boiled eggs, or L. Frank Baum's Mo, where chocolate caramels grow, and even the dragons have raspberry juice in their veins. No wonder autumn is so exciting: every good garden is ripe for the picking. Who could resist?

These days I am virtually a master, walking the streets of London with manila pay-packet envelopes in my bag. It's a familiar cycle: I seal the envelope, stuff a few extras in my pocket. Some are cursed to face the washing machine; the rest, now a prickly patty of seeds, pocket fluff and coins, are safely put away: I won't bother with labelling, I decide. I'll definitely recognise them.

Months later the crumpled packets, filled with unknowable husks and black bits, could be tithonia or artichoke or sunflower. Sick of the lot of them, I scatter their remains about the garden, where they invariably produce either hundreds of ordinary yellow Welsh poppies, or nothing at all.

LATE AUTUMN

'My whole life had been spent waiting for an epiphany, a manifestation of God's presence, the kind of transcendent, magical experience that lets you see your place in the big picture. And that is what I had with my first compost heap.'

Bette Midler, quoted in the *Los Angeles Times*
8 May 1996

I SMELL WINTER

I don't want to go outside. There are too many containers to wrap. I can't face the knuckle-aching cold; my annual failure to provide even semi-adequate drainage; the magazines' assumption that I could knock together a 'simple protective frame' of chicken wire and straw; the non-existence of tape sufficiently sticky to hold the crazed insulating patchwork together; the saucers of frozen leaf mulch I will inevitably pour on my socked feet; the intimations of plant death. The olive and lemon verbena do not realise the danger they face but, like a Somme doctor, I jolly them along: 'Chin up, Tommy; I'm sure you'll be back on your foot, feet, by Christmas.'

My plants are freezing, their roots soggy and desperate, and I don't want to go outside.

To add to the fun, the viburnum is scattering its dead leaves all over the main bed, like Gothic confetti. Even I, with my capacity for leaf love, can find little in these hard-wearing dull brown crisps to admire, but at least they provide the slugs with much-needed shelter. Rakes, even elegant hand-rakes, are useless in a space so small and thickly planted. The leaves, which otherwise would suffocate my tiny 'Sugar Loaf' seedlings, must be pinched up individually. Then I pack them in pierced sacks, water them and, because I'm so short of space, hide this precious leaf-mould-in-waiting by the compost bins, where I tread on it daily until I remember and unwrap the sodden squidge, useless for much except, yes, adding to the compost bin.

This is the point in the year's time-honoured cycle when the good gardener clears and tidies and prepares for winter, to be ready for the new life which will follow. Barry must be emptied of mildewed coir and barbecue briquettes and rusted-shut cake tins and wire grilles and nameless papery bulbs and the economy teabags I bought to acidulate water for the blueberry and all the broken mugs I lied to myself might be useful and then forgot. I should wipe and dry the bamboo ends, wire-wool the dibber and trowel and loppers, dismantle and sharpen my secateurs and dip them in oily sand.

storing them far from overwintering slugs; scrubbing the illegible yet mysteriously persistent pencil from hundreds of plant labels; sorting through the old and disappointing seed packets. Given all my moaning about garden size, what excuse could I possibly have for not making this little patch of land ship-shape for future seasons?

And, most pressingly of all, I should be emptying the compost bin.

Love, as all country and western singers know, is never straightforward. I dread this job for weeks, piling up celery ends and cabbage cores and cardboard in whichever of the two is the current bin long after the point of decency, so the lid sits at a jaunty angle and the worms are looking liverish. When I peek into the maturer bin it looks beautifully ready, the surface scattered with undigested twigs and sewing thread and banana labels but rich and brown; my plants will love it. But the interim stage, the frozen hands and wet knees, the hours prostrated as I scrabble handfuls of compacted compost through the open hatch and throw it towards, sometimes into, a recycling bag, which must then be hauled over the pots which I have failed to move aside, so that we can start filling the now empty bin with kitchen waste while the other begins to ripen, hangs over me like a test of my gardening commitment, and every day I fail. Yet it is worth it, infinitely worth it, for the moment when, many hours after I started, with aching fingers but joy in my heart, I dump the last great gouts of black gold around my grateful redcurrants and at last hobble indoors, broken, radiant.

I adore compost, making compost, using compost, with a deep and ardent passion. Ugliness means nothing in a love object. My pair of bins are cheap council-subsidised black plastic; no timber beehive or rotating hot-box for me. They are feebly pierced for aeration and almost inaccessible behind the rough-barked multi-stemmed poky-twigged viburnum; merely reaching them gives one a sense of achievement. On cold days the contents gently steam. Sometimes I take off the lid, just to admire the rot.

Compost is an ordinary miracle. Once, on a trip to Kew Gardens, I insisted on a family viewing of the compost heaps: Andean foothills of detritus, baking-hot, steep-sided, inhabited by happy-looking rats. As a child I read a book called *McBroom's Wonderful One-Acre Farm*, American but illustrated by Quentin Blake, and its life lessons have never left me. The plot is *Babe* meets *The Grapes of Wrath*: the tale of a poor sharecropping family who buy farmland, only to discover that they have been cheated. Their 80 acres turn out to be stacked on top of each other like a pack of cards, and underwater. But, as all gardeners will immediately realise, pond silt is a blessing. Once the sun dries, the McBrooms' tiny farm is miraculously productive; corn grows enormous, spat-out watermelon seeds sprout in seconds and their evil neighbour tries to steal their magical soil by scraping it from his boots.

Among the underrated greats of children's literature which formed my infant mind – *The Phantom Tollbooth, Ramona, Professor Branestawm, The Land of Green Ginger, Fattypuffs and Thinifers* – none cast a more powerful spell than Sid Fleischman's ridiculous masterpiece. I now realise that my approach to gardening derives wholly from the adventures of WillJillHesterChesterPeterPollyTimTomMaryLarryandlittleClarinda. Fertility is everything. See the chocolatey crumb of my garden soil, rich as Christmas cake; the earthworms, too many to count? Isn't it as beautiful – whisper it, more beautiful – than any flower or fruit yet grown? And do you honestly think that shop-bought sacks of soil could have produced all this?

Of course not. The secret is compost: the object of a life's dedication. I compost everything. One day I will probably compost myself.

As Karel Čapek understood, owners of small town gardens don't have lawn mowings, hedge trimmings, pond silt, silage, mushroom compost or spent hops lying about for the taking. We would love beds sown with green manure, but they are already full of overwintering kale and raspberry runners and the possibly-still-alive prunings of fruit bushes, so we would need nail scissors to cut it and, even if I could choose between their myriad superpowers (nitrogen-fixing or soil structure? Winter tares or scarlet clover?) can it be worthwhile? Necessity is the mother of crazed improvisation. I snatch teabags almost before the tea is drunk, tearing each individually to release its leafy goodness. Egg shells, scrumpled newspapers and toilet-roll innards (outside bean-growing season); cardboard boxes, carefully stripped of bar codes; banana peel; dead tulips. Why stop there? My children, who beg for oven chips and microwave spaghetti carbonara, have chosen, in the broadest possible sense, the wrong home. Our fridge looks like the cold store in a medieval orphanage; it contains mysterious covered jugs, sinister seeping jars and muddy vegetables the size of heads. Everything requires washing, scraping, coring, chopping and then laborious cooking with interesting home-grown herbs before it even qualifies as a side dish. The kids may go hungry but who cares, when the vegetable peelings can go straight into the compost bin?

Once one starts looking, even a constrained urban life is rich with compostable possibility. How I miss our guinea pigs, for the armfuls of ammonia-soaked newspaper I cleared from their hutch every week, their little vegetable dung pellets. I have tried encouraging my god-daughter to adopt a pair; surely it's time she ditched her kitten? Don't stop there: what about the clots of mud on farmers' market carrots? The sweepings left after family haircuts; wood ash from the fireplace, enriched with scorched marshmallow crusts and perhaps not entirely coal-free, despite my careful monitoring? Even the most cursory country excursion leaves the car littered with wisps of wool, shreds of bark and fern, soft tufts of driftwood whose oceanic nutrients will sweeten the gooseberries. Maybe the sea near Fowey was particularly turquoise when we visited; I didn't notice. I was furtively stuffing seaweed into an empty water bottle.

I haven't finished. What of the contents of the dustpan, the tangles at the Hoover mouth, the lint from the tumble drier, always the same dusky lavender? Our quilt loses feathers; Hercules sheds fur, or is it the other way around? Either way, I am grateful. Certain productive corners of the house conceal cobwebby fluff balls ripe for the harvesting and, when reasonably sure no one will see me, I swoop, sometimes with a toy broom for improved reach. At least I'm not mad enough to pick satisfying clods of ancient dust from the spaces between the floorboards. Definitely not.

Wait, come back. A few years ago, I took my father on a stone-carving weekend at West Dean, for his birthday. He hated it; that's hardly the point. Now, when I arbitrarily decide to treat the brassicas to lime, I have simply to scrape it from the back of the horrible head I chiselled from cream-coloured Purbeck. I have tenderly rinsed wine and onion from a kilo of mussel shells. Coconuts are stripped of coir. My only sorrow is that, since leaving my job to write full time, I have lost not only the camaraderie of my colleagues but also the bags of still-steaming coffee-ground pucks I used to collect from the nearby greasy spoon and carry, almost wholly unembarrassed, up in the lift to the eleventh floor.

It gets worse. I have composted my godmother's tablecloth, my grandmother's napkins, moth-eaten cardigans, my own gardening jeans, so deeply impregnated with soil that, soaked, they would be a valuable source of nutrients, children's undergarments charity shops disdain. I frequently discover unrotted knicker elastic; as a crime-fiction reader it gives one a shock. The compost bins are becoming a sort of family archive, like a pet graveyard.

The great underrated writer Elizabeth Taylor describes Mrs Post of the Claremont Hotel throwing her 'small hair combings' out of the window: 'London birds, she had read, were short of nest-building materials.' What nonsense. London birds are horribly spoiled; it's my garden that needs our leavings. I snatch my daughter's hairbrush from her little hand; save every tangle of plughole hair, even nail-clippings. If blood, hoof and horn have a value, why not bits of me? Parenthood makes one relaxed about excretions, but gardening lowers the inhibitions even further. The nurses at a London hospital reputedly used to put tonsillectomy dressings on the beds; don't throw away that nosebleed-stained tissue. And did you know that urine is a great compost-accelerant? Well, yes, since you ask, we do have a toilet, but would you mind . . .

In the paradise of which I dream, pallet-loads of delectable peat-free compost, romantically based on biochar carbon or Herdwick sheep's wool or Lake District bracken, would be delivered, free, straight to the garden. Their home-made cousin is clumpy and unsievable, yes, but almost as magical. There is no greater smugness than making something out of nothing, food for plants you yourself have grown from seed. Even sifting through the warm claggy pile to rid it of cat-collar bells, teaspoons, earring butterflies, name tapes, pennies, inexplicably shiny nails, buttons, Kinder Egg components, broken china, shreds of tape, chocolate foil, pen lids, Lego, clothing labels, pennies and sequins is addictive.

'Just another five minutes,' you shout, as the sun sinks lower over the trellis, the moon rises and suddenly it's time for bed. How can one sleep, when there are still old avocado stones in need of crushing for another round of rot? Squash stems are the best of all, little nubs like babies' dried-up navels. If you really want to see a happy author, ignore readings and festivals and look for her in filthy denim in the garden, beating stale Christmas nuts into crumbs with a brick.

This is the forefront of scientific exploration. Let others prove the existence of gravitational waves; I am seeing how far one can push composting. Do rats prefer boiled rice? What about cooking oil? Isn't rubber natural? How long would terracotta crocks take to compost, or wooden spoons, or paperbacks? I pass a skip and eye the head-sized clods of ancient London clay, hauled by tired Poles from yet another basement excavation. Does that council bed really need quite so many bark chips or, indeed, flowers? What about clouds? Will I one day roam the streets with a shopping trolley, stealing vegetarian children?

Young people can be difficult to entertain. Why not entrance them with a demonstration of the care of compost worms? You could promise that, if they're good, they could gently lift a worm from the bucket of fresh compost, then shepherd it to the new bin-in-progress. Simple yet effective; Jae, a young Manhattanite lucky enough to help me was, well, awestruck. I don't think that's too strong a word.

I love my compost worms, as benign Quaker factory-owners once cherished their staff; as Lord Emsworth, leaning over the pig-pen gate, loved the magnificent Empress of Blandings. I recruited the original wrigglers myself, from among the ordinary garden earthworms; we were pioneers together. Then reinforcements arrived: a newspaper-wrapped handful of brandlings sent from the far north by a concerned family member with a poor view of my composting prospects. Many generations have passed since then; my livestock are now half-breed mongrel superworms, part Viking, cold-toughened, unusually hungry, disciplined and well-read.

Fiercely I protect my flock from extremes of moisture and dryness; I chop up sticks, remove excess lemon peel, and they repay me, in poo. When I find a colony frisking about inside a mango stone, or families nesting between sodden newspaper sheets, I feel like Tolstoy, admiring his happy serfs. Their writhing energy is astonishing, as are their sex lives. Compost-worms are enthusiastic hermaphrodites who mate by joining their clitella together before both exchanging sperm and laying eggs. It's adorable and very modern. They need no help from me but, if they ever do, I won't abandon them. I'll be pouring tiny glasses of liqueurs and scattering rose petals and, if the worst comes to the worst, I'm ready to lurk by the compost-bin lid with a syringe, trying to remember what I've read about giant pandas.

FACING FACTS

It is time to come in from the cold, make toast, briefly consider churning butter to go with it, reconsider, sit down firmly, jump up again to scare off a robin, sit down again, if necessary tie oneself to the chair and take a little time to contemplate one's mistakes.

What a ridiculous idea. If mistakes were straightforward, who would make them? I repeat the same disasters annually: forgetting to invest in Turkish rocket or a grafted mini-cucumber, planting too little dill and too many pot marigolds. Every year I decide not to buy a nursery-grown *Erigeron karvinskianus*, convinced that the clump I pull from a neighbouring wall will flourish and self-seed; it dies on the journey home. I still can't get the right salad-sowing timing. I still don't understand pruning.

And something must be done about fruit production. In his extremely dangerous *A Year at Otter Farm*, which manages to combine a passion for agretti and Siberian pea trees with, remarkably, a sense of humour, Mark Diacono writes, 'Blackcurrants make a genius of any gardener.'

Diacono is a man I trust; he is the only person I have ever met who loves mulberries as much as I do. So what goes wrong with my blackcurrants? The Royal Horticultural Society claims that one blackcurrant bush should yield about 4.5 kilograms of fruit. There are few birds here, because of the cats, but might some very tiny ones be lurking, in disguise, to steal my currants? Or is the truth much more humiliating: do I grow hardly any in the first place? They were dosed weekly with liquid tomato feed and teaspoonfuls of wood ash, like Roo's Extract of Malt in *Winnie the Pooh*; I banished every slug and sawfly, crooned to them, watered them with my tears, yet the yield was ludicrously small. Should I have planted them closer together or further apart? Was the problem the inevitable underplanting, or poor variety selection or some other schoolgirl error? Should I not have squashed those caterpillars?

Not everything was technically my fault. Take this straggly little bush, labelled 'Rovada Redcurrant 1 litre'. Look carefully. You see those strange baubles among the leaves: a lunar-transparent whitish-green like snail eggs, with pink seeds suspended in the jelly? Which, in their first year, anyone would assume were unripe redcurrants, and wait and wait until the currants became no redder, but wizened on the vine? Yes, those ones. They're whitecurrants. What about my lovely amelanchier, bought for its fruit but increasingly recommended in the press for its prettiness, its reliability and its autumn colour; how could anything fed that much manure, loved so consistenty, look so jaundiced?

And it's all very well telling novice fruit growers to invest in walk-in galvanised steel fruit cages, with finials and storm clips, or to build their own. I tried, stretching metres of cheap netting over prickly bushes, propping it up with a ragged collection of hoop-shaped canes and interesting branches, whose flower-pot toppers refused to stay in place thanks to their drainage holes and which, despite ingenious weighing-down with bricks and logs, proved to offer birds an ideal enviroment for picnicking. Without spatial-awareness, gardening can be a torment. Pruning, for example; lacking a patient and expert teacher, I have to rely on pictures, yet the moment I turn to one, whether straightforwardly photographic or soothingly two-colour, helpfully enhanced with arrows, dotted lines and imaginative cross-hatching, my mind judders to a stop. Certain words – lateral, central leader, basal cluster, spur – seem to act as verbal coshes. My white redcurrant came with a calm and concise leaflet, encouraging me to prune the leading shoots, shorten the branch leaders, then spur prune young lateral growths. Sorry? The Royal Horticultural Society Wisley Handbook, *Grapes Indoors and Out*, contains sentences such as: 'In the second summer train vertically the two rods, keeping all other shoots pinched back to two or three leaves and then tie them horizontally at leaf-fall.' Individually the phrases make a sort of sense but then, as if my mind were an Etch A Sketch, it sweeps completely clear.

The same applies to propagation: it's all very well saying 'take hardwood cuttings' but what, and how? And where, again? However often I fold over magazine pages and buy helpful manuals, at the mention of cutting horizontally in the direction of growth above a basal node my mind seems to freeze like a lake in a time-lapse video: crystals to pack-ice in half a second flat.

This year's disasters also include virtually criminal acts of carelessness: the seed of an overpriced custard apple, hoarded, miraculously germinated, tenderly potted out and then, because I left it unlabelled, confident that I'd remember it, mistaken for a weed and beheaded. Another victim was this year's only full-sized acorn squash, whose iron shell and elegant stripes I admired for months until, clearing 'Tromboncino' stems in the half-light, I accidentally ripped the entire plant from the soil. No one in their right mind would plop the torn roots back in the soil, pat them down and then walk away casually, hoping that the plant wouldn't notice. Purely theoretically, I can tell you that the whole thing would wilt before you reached the back door; you'd have to snip off the lower half of the stem and leave the top dangling from the cane to which it was tied, in the hope that the poor fruit would ripen anyway.

It won't. I mean, it wouldn't.

As for clematis, if I gave the impression that I learned to avoid them after the long-ago roof-terrace debacle, I lied. The minute we had taken possession of this garden I bought two new ones, planted them deeply and mulched them thickly, avoiding the root exposure from which their predecessors may have suffered: look how much I had learned! Months later, their nursery tags long buried, with no idea of when they blossomed because only the neighbours over the trellis ever saw the flowers, I found myself in a herbaceous pruning group hell. They need a good corrective clipping but a latent clematis looks very like dried-up sticks. Every time I clear dead leaves and twigs nearby, I find a thicket of stubborn stems and it is only when I notice the furry grey-green leaf buds in my hand that I realise, once again, this may be a bad year for clematises.

This time last year, Forest Gardening seemed the answer to all my troubles. After half an hour with the magnificent *Plants For A Future*, by bus-driver-turned-edible-perennial-god Ken Fern, I had fallen, hard, for a life of yellow asphodel, northern fox grapes and quamash bulbs. You must read this book, for its sense of humour, its warmth, its expertise and intelligence; see, if you doubt me, the entry for house leek. I long to sit at the feet of Joy Larkcom but, to have a hope of post-apocalyptic survival, I mean to befriend Ken.

However, in modest gardens, perennial vegetables, like babies, aren't as straightforward as one might assume. Pignuts may be an ingenious solution to global food shortages, but I mistook my single plant for a carrot, and pulled it up. Once one has planted Jerusalem artichokes, they're there for life; mine, however, have vanished. There is only so much one can do with a solitary nodding onion. Of course I have lovage; once a season a leaf or two adds a faintly unpleasant something to minestrone. No one will admit it but chard is horrible, like sweet succulent metal. I have found a single recipe which suits it, a vaguely Lebanese soup with lentils and cumin and plenty of lemon; otherwise, spare me the disappointment.

This year the 'Violetto de Chioggia' artichoke, after years of non-production, suddenly decided to dazzle. Three flower heads appeared; in my excitement I visited them daily, admiring them until the edible buds of the larger two had blossomed into iodine-coloured thistly beauties. It was time to accept the inevitable and cut them to bring indoors yet, again, I missed the moment, allowing them to fade and die where they stood, unregarded except by me. The survivor, boiled and dressed with vinaigrette, tasted like a prickly little cat's-paw: mainly -choke, and very little arti-. Help me, Ken; I'm getting hungry.

The more I learn, the worse things become. I would go to the wall for Radio 4, even if Moneybox Live seems to air twenty-four hours a day. Today, like a miracle, I turned it on to find *Gardeners' Question Time*: discussions of *Tetrapanax papyrifer*, pansies and mini-diggers, how to make fleece hoops out of bicycle wheels and vanquish purple algae. The gentle laughter of the English middle classes is a lovely sound.

Then I heard something ominous. Containerised plants, a panellist re-marked, need far greater root space than we assume. Take, he said, tomatoes.

(I put down my coffee.)

How much space, he asked, as the interested murmuring reached a higher pitch, do you think a single plant needs?

(By now I was holding my breath; I had put my hand over the top of my favourite mug, featuring Mr T from *The A-Team*, in case, surprised, I knocked it over.)

I'll tell you, he said. It's a cubic metre.

This is a disaster. I must change my ways, yet again; after all that effort to limit container numbers, the small ones given away, the offerings from friends resisted, I need *more* pots, more space, some capillary matting and probably an automatic watering system. It's all I can do to sit here typing; think of the drip-hoses I must research. Gardening, I remember, is a bottom-less pit of money and time, a sump, a spittoon, a cruel and profligate mistress and every failure, each rebuff, merely goads me to try harder, be better. I pray it never ends.

LOOKING UP

Brunswick Square Gardens is one of those public spaces one hurries through, averting one's eyes from its dusty hebes, pigeon feathers, sandwich packaging and attention-seekers doing tai chi in loose-fitting shorts. Yet this morning, for the first time in twenty-two years, I chanced to look up.

Views pass me by. 'It's a lovely day,' everyone says and I will lift my head, surprised. Give me assorted pebbles on a beach, even a stony field and, like a particularly stupid dog, I'll be happy for hours. Gravel the size of unshelled mixed nuts is my favourite: flints and quartz, bits of belemnite, devil's toenails and other fragments of minor fossils, of nugatory value except to me. Even where prehistoric remains are unlikely, there is usually something worth seeing at ankle height: an interesting manhole cover, groundsel or chickweed, the silhouette of a hydrangea leaf imprinted on the pavement.

So, while any sane person gazes about as they walk through London's parks, I keep my head down. But the tree I noticed today was extraordinary: gigantic, swollen and mottled as a moulting bison. The trunk had split; its unpollarded lower branches barely skimmed the heads of passers-by as above it rose a beautifully rounded crown, like an afro. Against the bright blue sky of a perfect English winter morning, a handful of yellow leaves shivered and spun, making the spherical fruit which hung from every branch look as silly as badly chosen earrings.

In this city we tend to ignore London planes. They are giants in camouflage sleeping bags: on parade along Chelsea Bridge Road, bulging threateningly in St Pancras Gardens opposite the old hospital, filling the air of Fitzrovia with uvula-irritating bristly achenes which race along the pavements, blown by exhaust fumes, like wildebeest galloping beneath a helicopter.

Trees are extremely, discreetly, strange. We think of plants as knee height, shrubs or flowers, something to look down upon. They're bizarre in their own right – the cells that know to grow in straight lines or frills, the orange and purple and green – but, if you heard of a distant land where redcurrant bushes and basil grew to the size of buildings, wouldn't you want to see? Then think of the fractal weirdness of plant growth: leaf veins splayed like tiny boughs, stems like shrunken tree-trunks. Think of your own arteries, the branching of your lungs, then look up at a naked wintry beech tree: a mammoth among mice.

But was this tree beautiful? The bulging bark under its older branches looked like sagging human flesh. I managed to stand still enough to watch its flower-heads trembling in the faintest of breezes, the Euston Road wind-tunnel filtered by the Brunswick Centre's neo-Brutalist concrete balconies. The tourists and buses seemed to fall silent, leaving the tree the only point of calm. No one else was looking at it; what fools, to be oblivious to the wonder in their midst. Then I read the sign beside the gate and discovered that, irritatingly, others have noticed it before me. It is the Brunswick Plane, designated a Great Tree by expert judges after the great Hurricane of 1987. I looked back at the tree; yes, I decided. Definitely beautiful, after all.

THE SLIPPERY SLOPE

It is traditional to bring unwise items back from holidays: mosaic coffee tables. Herbal liqueurs. Novelty salad servers. I would never do such a thing. The appalling fuss my children made when I insisted on bringing a handsome blue and white Greek feta cheese tin home in their suitcase was completely unreasonable. Yes, it was a metre or so tall, but it was also hollow, so could easily be stuffed with shorts and jelly shoes and all those interesting family quiz books we had ignored all week. I'm sure that the café owner was laughing out of friendliness. And you hardly noticed the sheepy smell on our T-shirts. Admittedly on drizzly London brick the effect was less Aegean terrace than kebab-shop, so I put the tin out of sight, on top of the shed, while I debated whether to plant it with Sicilian-widow crimson pelargoniums or something for colder, wetter summers, like swede. It was perfectly safe, until the tiny electrician we had asked to fix the outside light decided to stand on it, utterly crushing my object of beauty. It's heartbreaking. Like the zinc box from the local junk shop, and the plastic wine-making barrel abandoned on the pavement, and the rusted fire bucket I found in a hedge, it had so much potential.

Everything is irresistible to a gardener but the greatest thrill comes from the almost totally blameless theft of objects others have abandoned. Look at this exciting glass demijohn; if I could work out how to remove the bottom with a combination of boiling water and ice, it would make a bell jar, for free. When it's too cold to plant, finding garden treasure is a marvellous distraction. I once discovered a huge liver-coloured crate on a nearby pavement; judging by its strange lino-like texture and the scribbles around the edge, it had obviously once stored confidential files for a local spymaster. It was wonderful; for an entire year I used it as a presumably toxic trough for salad, until my family forcibly took it away.

No matter if the wood-and-iron sledge I bought at a car-boot sale is too heavy to use for sledging on Parliament Hill; it's a perfect crutch for the abutilon. Never mind if the comfrey liquid I make in the plastic barrel reeks, and its tap is blocked with rotting leaves; give me two minutes and it'll be good as new. Raffia may one day come in handy, and pipe-cleaners, and some of this immense pile of corks. Of course I want that thick sheet of Perspex, and that cooling rack is definitely useful, and could I use that broken car-mirror to reflect natural light on my seedlings? Yes please, I'll have that empty plastic water bottle; they make excellent incubators. Just because I keep cutting myself while sawing them in half with a bread knife, and they attract slugs, and don't actually work, doesn't mean I shouldn't try.

Maybe Derek Jarman would have rejected the big plastic salad bowl Gabrielle left out for the bin-men but that's only because he lacked the vision to use it as a geodesic basil dome. I am past caring. When does a harmless compulsion tip over into lunacy? I fear we may be approaching that point as swiftly as one can, when weighed down with beach stones and broom handles and the legs of a children's easel and this probably invaluable wicker basket.

NOT GARDENING

Snow should still be exciting. Nature has nothing else remotely like it: no dense layer of raindrops, no silently falling golden flakes of sun. It muffles the roar of double-decker buses, tempts the most modern child outdoors and, temporarily, masks city grot, like an anxious baker embracing icing.

Last night's snowball fight has left great brownish sweeps through that beautiful marshmallow fluff, reminding me of the havoc taking place at ground level: blackening and snapping. Rot. 'I'm just . . .' I say, vaguely gesturing at the garden, opening the door. Even before I've found my galoshes, the fuss is unbelievable. It's not as if it's still snowing, yet my family insist on prioritising their silly old physical comfort. How can they resist the unobstructed sight of the garden, the wholesome air?

Still, I need my fix. Gazing through smeary glass won't do it. It's gardening-time; only when it starts to hail, and I'm turning blue, will I retreat to a hot bath, seed catalogue and a rollerball suitable for vertical writing.

But like toddlers, gardeners should never be left to bathe alone. We pretend to read a page or two of our novel, put it down, casually pick up a catalogue. A simple photograph, the most cursory description and our veins are pulsing with adrenaline, dopamine, desire. What will it be next year? The delicious but tricky 'Brandywine' tomato; the demented 'Reisetomate Pocketbook', each fruit a gorgeously deformed bobbly cluster? Whisper to me of chestnut roses; beach plums; *Origanum vulgare* 'Compactum', Beth Chatto's favourite. Have I already missed the last available packet of 'Lemon Drop chilli (rare)'? I might just leave a message on the nursery's answerphone.Filling out the order form merely quickens my thirst. The urge to run downstairs now, in my towel, and into the garden, is growing harder to contain.

Garlic cress. *Cautleya cathcartii* 'Tenzing's Gold' BSWJ 2281 perennial ginger. Short-toothed mountain mint, daylily 'George Cunningham'. Dr Wyche's Yellow tomatillo. Rocket 'Dragon's Tongue'. Giant chives.

Let it snow.

EARLY WINTER

'The declining winter sun...throbbed like a
sallow lemon on the westering lip of Mockuncle
Hill . . . High up, a few chalky clouds doubtfully wavered
in the pale sky that curved over against the rim of the
Downs like a vast inverted pot-de-chambre.'

Stella Gibbons, *Cold Comfort Farm*

NEVER MIND THE
BUTTERCRUNCH

When the buttercrunch lettuce has wizened and the rocket has keeled over, when every other salad green has deserted you, one stalwart remains: Asian greens.

Don't be frightened. They are easy to grow, hardy, productive and exciting. Try komatsuna, with its shiny leaves and juicy pale stems which taste like the best bits of cabbage and spinach and mustard combined; mizuna and mibuna, the highlights of any supermarket salad bag; perennial yet exciting kai laan, of which every part can be eaten; the ornamental kales, as seen in municipal flower-beds, ruffled or ridged or serrated, which add blasts of white, violet and red cosmic loveliness to salads; hon tsai tai, a hardy variety of choi sum, my favourite Chinese-restaurant vegetable, whose stems are purple, leaves green and flowers yellow, like something devised by Edward Lear.

Yet, even as I worship at the feet of these glorious vegetables, intriguing raw and delicious cooked, peppery and juicy and beautiful, I wonder whether, if they were also, say, Dutch, would they seem as tempting? Do Chinese and Japanese gardeners find our vegetable names, cabbage 'Avoncrest' and Brussels sprout 'Roger', parsnip 'Tender and True', as evocative, redolent of ice and gold and steel, as green-in-snow, Osaka purple mustard; yellow pak choi, shungiku greens or nine-headed bird?

My first taste of shungiku greens was in a bag of leaves from a farmers' market deep in the English countryside. The stallholder was Japanese; after a week of bed-and-breakfast fry-ups and pub dinners, the sight of her jars of miso made my stomach rumble. As I ate the flowering shoots and amaranth leaves with my fingers, feeling the scurvy recede, we chatted; chances to show off my oriental brassica vocabulary are sadly rare. Then I came to a new flavour: tangy, slightly bitter, floral, and knew that I would have to investigate this odd vegetable. The stallholder explained; it was shungiku, also known as chop suey greens, a type of edible chrysanthemum. With her faintly terrified blessing, I vowed to grow it myself.

It tastes, to be honest, exactly as chrysanthemums smell: aromatic, dry, like licking a cardboard box in a florist's, or a little worse. One taste is fascinating. Two, and one begins to flag. And, when one eventually manages to rear a full-sized plant from seed and then, after nibbling leaves and daisy-petalled flowers, one decides to leave the rest for another day, the result will be a 30-centimetre-high, scrawny, grey-green eyesore whose greenery will be too bitter to eat. It was a marvellous idea, but now I have a lifetime's supply of self-seeded chrysanthemum and don't even know the original stallholder's name, to blame her.

ON BEING A BAD GARDENER

Actually, it is all Joy Larkcom's fault.

Winter is the guilty season. We claim we love our gardens, cannot tear ourselves away and yet, when the rain is lashing the patio and unwanted plastic pots rattle at the foot of every drear and sluggy plant, there is always something to do inside, in the warmth. All the jobs we have left undone, out of ignorance or laziness – gooseberry-pruning, honeysuckle-trimming, mastering the dark arts of bud-grafting – lurk in the shadows, muttering reproachfully. Gardens seem to make even non-gardeners feel some sort of shame or sense of failure; they don't know what to do with all those overgrown trees, or where to start with their new bare flower-beds. Books have exactly the same effect; ask anyone if they read much fiction and, ten to one, they'll tell you, a bit shifty or bashful, that they should read more. Gardening ought to be about the joy of new life, the quivering of our excited senses, not lists of chores and homework undone, so many cold and nasty tasks.

Take, for example, washing and disinfecting seed trays. It is desperately important to avoid damping-off. I never do it. Does it honestly matter, if the seeds still happily grow? Unlike our gardening forebears, few of us sterilise leaf mould in the oven; with luck, seed-tray-washing will soon slip out of fashion too. I apply the same haphazard logic to seedling spacing and crop rotation: guarding my progeny, tending them, loving them and then squishing the lot into tiny spaces higgledy-piggledy and hoping it'll toughen them up. Crop rotation used to torment me. I spent hours trying to draw diagrams of my so-called beds divided into the traditional families, brassicas, legumes, onions, roots and potatoes, certain that, if I disobeyed this basic principle, my yields would suffer. Who knows if they did? Rotation on such a miniature scale would be absurd for anyone; for me, unable to work out how five groups change place on a four-year cycle, it would be fatal. Nowadays, when I finally haul out of the soil whatever intensively harvested brassica has occupied the same patch of soil for several years, I simply try to plant its replacement a little to the left.

If it hadn't been for Joy Larkcom, gardens like mine wouldn't exist. Her combination of calm intelligence and passionate curiosity liberated British gardeners from long rows of sprouts and carrots, made us begin to see the ornamental potential of edibles despite the edicts of the men on the television. That we now grow mixed cut-and-come-again salad leaves, mizuna and kai laan, pea shoots and purslane, is largely her doing; directly or via other writers, she has influenced almost every vegetable choice I have made. However, this doesn't mean Joy would approve of my gardening. She'd probably despair of my piecemeal planting, the low pollination and scrappy appearance of what I secretly think of as my potager. I have never produced a single glossy patch of Batavia Red lettuce, let alone a wheel effect with Salad Bowl Green between the spokes. Anyone who has crossed Europe in a campervan, gathering Portuguese red peas, black radishes and edible lupins, must be prudent, and thrifty; when she leafs through the catalogues I suspect that she wastes no time drooling over Sundries, dreaming of precision seeders for £163.25, pruning saws, plant theatres, log stores, rainbow wipe-clean labels, glass bell cloches, trumpet-shaped plant supports, top-of-the-range aluminium cold frames, pre-assembled watering kits and scarifying rakes. People without lawns probably don't need lawn-aerating shoes. I bet Joy's soil is perfect without rock dust or liquid humic acid; she must, by now, be immune even to the wiles of the Felco manufacturers. I am weak, and ashamed. When I hear myself murmuring 'phwoaar' at the sight of plastic grafting clips (colour may vary), I know that I am letting myself down, letting my garden down but, worst of all, letting down Joy.

STILL LIFE

Of all her publications, Joy Larkcom's *Salad Garden*, republished as *The Organic Salad Garden*, is the one you most urgently need. So few gardening books work on several levels at once, instructing and stimulating both amateur and expert, explaining, calmly, clearly, the point of watering and when to gather wild salads, which edible flowers taste best and why you should always cut a cross on a cabbage stump to make it regrow.

Even better, it has portraits of lettuce. If you grow and cook vegetables with any degree of passion, you begin also to fall in love with their beauty: the translucent orange of a slice of 'Burpee's Golden' beetroot, the deep dark gloss of a Red Verona chicory leaf. Yet most gardening books, until recently, ignored this. Larkcom, with the help of the botanical photographer Roger Phillips, blasted through this convention. Do you want to spot the differences between oriental bunching onion 'Ishikura', giant chives, standard chives, Welsh onions, spring onions, Chinese chives and Chinese chives in bud? I certainly do. Have you seen the roots on those self-blanching celeries? Look at these Japanese radish cross-sections: I could gaze at them all day.

This year the National Gallery will hold an exhibition of Dutch flowers. It is free, but I am worried. How many times are individuals allowed to go? Twice? Three times? More? What will happen to those of us who cannot keep away; will the guards nod kindly? Will they whisper? Also, about the merchandise: what if it's all room-fragrance diffusers and fudge and freesia hand cream? Some of us are made of stronger stuff: if we can't have an actual Rachel Ruysch, we want A1-sized posters of Ambrosius Bosschaert the Elder's every rotting cyclamen leaf; *Sunset Boulevard*-style close-ups of plum bloom. It isn't the colour but the exactitude we crave: the precision of their dew drops, their rigid lobsters, their marigolds like shaggy wilting suns.

Rory McEwen, my favourite artist, was the heir of the masters, of Willem van Aelst and Jan van Huysum, yet broke new ground. Painting on vellum, with minute brushes and a penknife, he captured photographically, no, better than in a photograph, the fragile rigidity of a snake's head fritillary stem, the buff and rose and plum and vermillion of an Indian onion; dried chillies and oak leaves on the turn.

'I paint flowers,' he wrote, 'as a way of getting as close as possible to what I perceive as the truth, my truth of the time in which I live.'

Even better, McEwen appreciated rot. I have loved him fruitlessly for most of my life, since first seeing his *True Facts from Nature* series as an easily moved teenager. His understanding of decay is palpable; you can smell it in 'Onion' (1975), in each flopping tulip, in every crumbling leaf. On reflection, the National can keep its Ruysches. All I want is a McEwen: a small one would do.

GETTING MY KICKS

O ne does what one can. We may hide from the boggy frost-blackened hell of our real-life gardens, but those of us who are truly obsessed need to get through the long winter somehow.

When I worked in an office, I relied on two sources of vegetable thrills; I used to visit them in my lunch breaks. One, a horrible florist, was inevitably focused on window boxes for city-dwellers. Wistfully I would caress the sale shelf, the tiny lurid privets and black witchy *Ophiopogon planiscapus*, shrublets covered in miniature faux oranges, trays of pansies as brutally reared as veal calves. Why, I would wonder repeatedly, like a wistful dimwit in a Seventies French film roaming a garden in flattering cheesecloth, don't they sell seeds? Oh yes, we're in central London. What monster invented petite azaleas? Does someone dye those kalanchoes to make them even uglier? This is depressing. I miss my garden. Why don't they sell seeds?

The other was the world's most expensive grocery shop, attached to a cheese emporium. Although the cheese room itself was godly, like a family mausoleum made of Taleggio and Pont-l'Évêque, one sniff made my sandwiches seem even sadder. I focused on the greengrocery section: the Sicilian lemons, ugly and therefore beautiful; fresh Coco de Paimpol beans, their pods ropy-looking but the beans like smooth tight pearls; heavy heads of 'Pain de Sucre' chicory; *cime di rapa* turnip greens still beaded with the dew of Tuscan morns. I wanted it all; I couldn't afford a thing, but merely being in the presence of nature soothed and stirred me, simultaneously.

Sometimes a simple horticultural word is almost as good. What gardener on dull train journeys doesn't turn hungrily to the mail-order leaflets for Orchard Fruit Patio Ballerina Tree Collections and heavy-duty polytunnels which fall from strangers' newspapers? The other day, after a gruelling morning of making things up, I sat in the British Library eating my packed lunch and reading Elizabeth David's *Spices, Salt and Aromatics*, because that is what I do for fun and, amid the recipes for honey pie and brined beef, the words 'sesame seeds ... seeds of the plant *Sesamum indicum*' give me a little burst of excitement. How hard could it be to grow sesame plants? Next spring, shouldn't I try?

If you can find the perfect armchair garden-reading, it will soothe you better than almost anything other than really desolate Icelandic crime fiction. When it comes to comfort, personal preference is unpredictable. You may love the arch asides of Christopher Lloyd, or return, in times of trouble, to the black and white formality of double-digging and measured drills. You may like your magazines smart or scruffy, packed with gentry or allotmenteers. My own choice might surprise you; it certainly amazes me. It is *Mother Earth*, the quarterly journal of the Soil Association, for the years Winter 1949–October 1971 inclusive. Unexpectedly good-looking, with elegant typesetting and bound in bright leaf and rust and sky blue, each edition offers important articles on Pest Control in Nova Scotia, Reports to Members on Municipal Silage, photographs of prize-winning organically reared barley at Royal Horticultural Shows of the Sixties ... surely you're tempted? Look: here's a chemical analysis of Channel Island seaweed; how can you resist?

I know, I almost envy myself. Yet I had owned them for half my life, without understanding my amazing good luck. How we laughed when, at a student party, I was given them as a hilarious birthday present: a bale of booklets from a charity shop, tied with twine. Recycling hadn't been invented; I put them in a box with my lecture notes about ecclesiastical reform in the Second Bulgarian Empire, and gratefully forgot about the whole boring lot for two decades.

But to everything there is a season and, at last, the time came for the clearing of the boxes, to make space for my father's ever-growing collection of spare watch-straps and books of Latin insults. My bin bag at the ready, I flipped open the top copy and was transfixed. It contained a Member's Portrait and Biographical Note; 'A Doctor's Viewpoint of Wholefood'; a three-page poem entitled 'Scabby Apples'; an extremely technical study of African Soil Erosion; 'Earthworms and the Gardener' by Vice-Admiral Vivian; letters ('Should we have a badge?'; 'New York Milk Supplies'); Your Autumn Reading (*The Pioneering Pig*) and, most splendidly of all, a dispatch ('Letter from Australia No. 7') about the astonishingly lengthy global excursions of Lady Eve Balfour, with detailed accounts of hospitality enjoyed in the homesteads of Ulooloo with the Misses Wien-Smith.

By now I was in the best of reading places, the bath: sated, happy, but rather cold. As I looked for a towel, something printed on pale blue paper fell out of July 1964 and floated beside my shin: Members' Notes. The apparently sole retailer of organic food in London ('we can deliver by Post or Rail to the Provinces') urgently required compost-grown tomatoes; a new address was needed for The Hon. A. Bampfylde, Box 67, Nyeri, Kenya; Miss Hyder, 199 Piccadilly, W.1., had joined the Association; a Sussex member's house cow (excellent quiet milker) was available for loan or possible sale; an erratum slip announced the news that 'Members will be sorry to hear of the death of F. Newman Turner on holiday in Germany'; and, in the classifieds, Young Men sought work as market gardeners in non-fluoridated areas.

My shoebox of journals is a historical goldmine, a testament to the single-minded endeavour of brave, if hilariously posh, pioneers, yet I barely notice. Just as all my favourite crime writing has merged into a great morass of alcoholism, madness, deceit and unpleasant weather conditions, so too I have lost track of the cider apples and crop-spraying and worm casts. Haven't I read 'Dr J Swaby on Soil Fungi: Some Findings of Importance to Organic Husbandry' before? The second time around, Mrs Ethelyn Hazell's account of the difficulties of ciné-filming the Devonshire County Show leaves me almost unmoved. Isn't that photograph of weatherproof stooking in Ireland familiar? The winter evenings fly by. Give me a bath and a good long article on 'The Natural Control of Vertebrate Pests of Agriculture' (July 1959) and life is almost bearable.

MIDWINTER

'Comfrey: the whole plant is intensely interesting.'

Dorothy Hartley, *Food in England*

INDOOR GARDENING

Despite repeated checking, not one of my seed-sowing calendars can suggest anything to plant. Outside, everything is browned and sodden and nibbled; the pot-wrappings keep the slugs warm and energetic, like racehorse blankets, so they can frolic all night without discomfort. The soil I spent the year enriching is escaping over the top of my hopeless brick barrier; the hellebores have disappeared; brown water with the plaquey smell of toothbrushes fills every ignored saucer, waiting for its chance to spill into my galoshes. It's time to make bread.

As Margaret Costa wrote in the *Four Seasons Cookery Book*, baking bread makes 'the baker see herself in an almost biblical light as a valiant woman whose children shall rise up and call her blessed'. Normal yeasted bread is marvellous for making oneself feel saintly but, if one is a twitchy gardener, only sourdough will do. There is absolutely nothing in this life as satisfying as having made an actual loaf of bread oneself, using yeast one has harnessed from the air. Merely the thought of starting a sourdough culture – the wild yeasts, location-specific; the organic bitty flour; the stirring and sniffing and waiting – will make the horticulturally frustrated heart beat faster. Reviving an existing Stiltony jar-full makes one feel like a magician. Then the fun begins.

My favourite bread, a hard-core grainy Danish rye, takes two days; it is grown, not kneaded. I have recently been led to understand that everyone else would prefer Hovis Soft White; I will ignore this. Do they think I enjoy pottering about the kitchen, lightly dusted with flour, using my exciting wooden baker's peel and inventing interesting combinations of sultanas and fennel seeds? Absolutely not. I'm only thinking of their health.

Yet, like all obsessives, even in my selfless devotion I am unsatisfied. I long for just one entirely home-generated loaf. This year I accidentally produced a full-sized wheat plant, from a grain which had escaped our late guinea pigs, Tufty and Phoebe. I guarded it ferociously, watched it expand and ripen until it was harvest time. My traditional skills did not end there. Next I separated the grain from the chaff, by standing in a breeze with the oats in a bowl and wiggling my fingers about until the whispery florets floated obligingly away, although not, puzzlingly, the sharp little husk. The bowl was much emptier; only six genuine wheat grains, or possibly groats by now, remained. Even I could acknowledge they would be no use for bread. I put them in a newly established jar in the kitchen, beside several dried cannellini beans; I am working towards an entire meal's worth.

My adventures in microleaves and sprouted seeds have ended in sorrow and mould. It may be because the only spare kitchen surface was the dark corner by the wooden spoons, or because hippies are not to be trusted, but within days everything was both smelly and dry; I give up. Still, I must have something to grow. Is it time for house plants? Not quite yet: they are fussy, fleshy yet dry, naturally dusty-looking, rarely edible, the one form of plant life I have always found it easy to ignore. Until now. Since finding Tovah Martin's *The Unexpected Houseplant* on a charity-shop bookshelf I have begun to feel a sense of urgency about succulents. The ceaselessly reproducing aloe vera I accepted in an unguarded moment from the butcher appeals to my neurotic-homesteader tendencies; it's good for burns which, come the apocalypse, might be handy. I have recently begun to understand the appeal of house leeks. Yesterday I took a step in the wrong direction, buying a small rosary vine, *Ceropegia woodii*, from the garden centre I happened to pass, thanks to a very long short cut, on my way home. It came in a horrible white plastic hooked contraption; I suddenly understand macramé. I have draped its small silvered kidney-bean leaves over my bookshelves so that, every time I reach for an interesting reference book, I will knock it to its death.

Surely I'll be able to resist the lure of aspidistras and variegated spider plants for another year, I think, even as I try, once again, to manoeuvre one of my old roof-terrace wire window-box-holders over the sash-window top. Back goes the chair on the spare-bed mattress, the pots on top of that: a violent-looking *Sansevieria cylindrica* and a misleadingly named Himalaya sedum 'Tornado'; six aloe babies, each scrappier and less succulent than the last. I tell myself that, unless I buy a painted china pot-holder, they're not really house plants; I'm just overwintering them until the spring.

My study is already the scene of furtive daytime tendernesses. A well-designed window box is a lovely thing: fuchsia, skimmia, delphiniums. Mine contains none of these; only a scruffy rosemary whose leaves I nibble to stimulate my mind; snowdrop and fritillary bulbs planted too shallowly for comfort; a slow-dying lavender; pinks, which taste like cloves, if one is far from the kitchen and desperate; a surprising amount of cat-grass; and my beloved, my darling, the seedling I grew from the stone in a dried beige unpromising Hunza apricot. But cold weather leads to reading and, with reading, come delusions. The bookshelves are growing dangerous: books about log-chopping, mushroom-gathering and warm wax seals for grafted apples; modern Irish salami; drawings of 'beef vegetables'; and Dorothy Hartley's clear-eyed and fearless descriptions of sheep-marking, the uses of parsnip leaves, how to salt a whole pig, when to harvest radish pods, the anatomy of mountain rams, roasting ptarmigans, feeding shepherds and Elizabethan lunches. Of course I want a pig. I have read of wartime Pig Clubs; the animals (Middle Whites, medium-sized and quiet) must have been kept in back gardens occasionally, even in London. I haven't yet worked out how to feed it while maintaining my compost levels; it hinges on whether vegetarian pigs' manure is usable, and how much I would have to pay Gabrielle to keep her from telling the council. I definitely don't want sheep, thanks to a traumatic experience on Dartmoor when, visiting friends, I recklessly offered to help with lambing and almost immediately found myself covered in uterine mucus before, at the sight of the work table (jumbo tubs of rubber castration rings; an ordinary pincushion, stuck with threaded needles), having to sit down rather quickly. But what about bees? Cousin Maurice could show me how, but is it a wise hobby for an easily distracted city-dweller? Shouldn't I simply buy a jar of honey and a bee veil and consider it a lucky escape?

My ambitions grow ever more deranged. How about yoghurt? That's alive, sort of, isn't it? I love the stuff, whether supermarket blackcurrant or Kurdish mountain-style, but isn't this just another excuse to buy equipment? Could I make soft cheese? And how long will I be able to resist the logical conclusion, which involves spending too much time on cheese-enthusiast websites, moving to the country, investing heavily in goats and wax and second-hand cheese-mills and straw mats and hundredweights, producing one small grey patty which no one will even be willing to try and eventually dying alone of cholesterol and bankruptcy and sorrow? I may be the only non-Irish person with nostalgia for carrageen pudding, made from *Chondrus crispus* plucked at low water from the icy seas off Ballyandreen. The Thames tide-line is probably not the best alternative; are London mosses out of the question? Shall we try lichen?

Here we go again. Every summer I swear to get a grip, to try fewer mad projects, rationalise my pots and halve the number of crops I grow so unsuccessfully yet, each winter, my resolve fails me. I have barely scratched the surface of the fruit and herbs and vegetables I want to grow. Can I face a future without Nepalese raspberries, lingonberries, cloudberries, boysenberries, worcesterberries, red valerian or golden hops or mooli or mashua or nashi or pineapple guavas? I honestly don't know that I can.

THE APPLES I HAVE LOVED

Of all the many reasons to worship Myrtle Allen, the great champion of Irish food, founder of the Ballymaloe cookery empire and evangelist for carrageen, the foremost is her *Ballymaloe Cookbook*, my desert-island cookery book and location of the most beautiful chapter heading ever written: 'The Apples I Have Loved.'

You may think that you too are a lover of apples; you are wrong. Munching on the odd Granny Smith does not grant you membership of this small but passionate sect. Joan Morgan, author of *The Book of Apples*, is our pin-up. She has tasted over two thousand varieties; imagine being her humble apprentice. I briefly went to school with her son and now torment myself by imagining a parallel universe, in which I was excused hockey in order to carry her briefcase on trips to the National Apple Collection at Brogdale in Kent.

Like Freemasons, we apple-lovers are quick to bond. I once passed a message to Inge, mother of my friend Tina, in praise of her delicious apple cake. Five A4 sheets of recipes arrived by return, including:

Hot

Swedish

Blackberry

Almond

Spiced

Jane's

French
Deep Dutch
Bavarian
Dorset
Irish
Open
and Plain.

We, well, I, eat so many apples that the fruit man at the market always re-
duces my bill, out of pity. Dog-walkers laugh as they pass me, struggling
home like a donkey in a charity advertisement. This is real devotion, or addiction, and 5 kilos of organic Worcesters and Russets do not come cheap.
Yet have you noticed how often garden-writers, indeed country-dwellers in
general, refer lightly to apple trees or even orchards? As if having the chance
to watch the blossom unfurl and the green marbles swell and ripen and then
to reach up and pick one, sun-warmed, rain-washed, fresh and pure and
entirely yours, is nothing special, no different to owning a lawnmower or a
shed? Aren't you gnashing your teeth at the thought of the casualness, the
waste? Do they appreciate each bite of those apples? And what about windfalls? Don't get me started. I'd be a class warrior, except that I'm holding out
my rucksack, looking hopeful. Come the revolution, I'll be consulting my
long list of possible varieties, trying to decide if their soil is good enough for
a St Edmund's Pippin.

Yet, conceivably, an actual functional apple tree is within even my peasant
reach. That viburnum; how, precisely, is it earning its keep? This is prime
blossom season and yet, for every two or three minute white and pink scented trumpets, there are twenty brown corpses in a clot of rot that crumbles
into dust at one's touch, like a dream flower.

Might there be, I mentioned at breakfast the other day, even the tiniest
argument for chopping it down and replacing it with something more,
well, normal? With healthy blossom and picturesque branches and edible
rewards?

The response was outraged but not technically violent. That would do. I
dropped my spoon and hared upstairs to commune with Joan Morgan and
the apple books, which understand me, which know that there are few more
magical phrases than 'still found in old gardens' and which hear music in the

words 'Sweetest of codlins and most colourful with slight red flush. Makes delicately flavoured baked apple. Widely grown C19th, especially in north, Scotland'.

Hours, days, later, I had narrowed the selection to fourteen; then, by acknowledging but not prioritising the pollination needs of my existing 'Orleans Reinette', to eight. As garden-writers sometimes publish lists of optimum trees for orchard-owners, I include my very useful notes, should you find yourself in a similar dilemma:

Sunset (very Cox)
Blenheim Orange (dual purp, vigorous, too like Orleans? Tricky?)
Lord Lambourne (James Grieve × Worcester Pearmain, compact, yum, good cropper)
Katy (also JG×WP; how does that work? SWEDISH)
Ashmead's Kernel (YUM but poor cropper. But online friends like. What to do?)
Ribston Pippin (Triploid) (???)
Tydeman's Late Orange (bit cox, good crop)
Discovery (I love)

And that was as far as I got. Still it seems to me that, if I learn this year to prune a cordon, and cut back the ivy, and buy a lorry-load of manure and get rid of Barry and the viburnum and almost everything else, I could have room for a small but emphatic orchard: at least two trees. And maybe a Ribston Pippin.

FANTASY

O r I could replace the viburnum with a mulberry tree.

I am furious that I don't have a mulberry. As you will have gathered, the legacies of my peculiar childhood are many and various and one of the most unfortunate is this: I am in love with mulberries. My father worked near a very productive tree; once a year he forced us to put on our oldest, and therefore smallest, clothes, and spend the afternoon spreading sheets and shaking branches. Then, looking like little murderers, we would return, mulberry juice dripping from our carrier bags as we pedalled wearily home. How we dreaded it; the humiliation, the scratches, the stomach ache. And now how I long to taste mulberries again, the juiciest and best of fruit, so richly sharp-sweet, like a raspberry taken to extremes. Mulberry fever is a curse. One remembers each tree ever encountered; I once secretly chose a Greek package holiday specifically because mulberries apparently grew in the main square. Fresh off the ferry, still seasick, I invented an errand so I could investigate, and found they were the wrong kind, white and sweet and pointless. On a walk in Kew Gardens one September I found a treeful; ignoring the infants wailing for drinks and plucking at my ankles, I picked until I could reach no more. But, as all mulberry-lovers know, they do not keep, not even for the journey home. My poor addicted father would feed the squashed survivors into bottles of sugared gin to last him until next year; I built mine a nest of newspaper and, like a birds-egg thief, brought them fifteen stops home on the train. The result wasn't pretty.

But that is not enough. I want, no, I need a tree of my own. I correspond with expert tree-growers about my vision of a container-grown tree; they all explain that mulberries root too shallowly to be stable in a container, and fruit slowly, and deserve to fulfil their potential in the ground. I don't listen. Every year the planting season passes, while I debate (with myself; no one else cares) size, and maturing time, and whether 'Chelsea' really descends from a single early famous tree and how much, romantically, that matters.

Of course, my garden is already a fantasy: the most expensive, time-consuming, undecorative and self-indulgent way to grow dinner imaginable. Yet I cannot stop. I still want a pond, for toads; an arbour; Parisian hotbeds; bantams; nectarines; a pergola hung with golden squashes, each a day away from perfection so they must be constantly watched but never picked. And this is how it should remain; an unfulfilled fantasy, never disappointing, always possible: a source of perfect, fruitful happiness.

ACKNOWLEDGEMENTS

Thanks to:

* Max Mendelson: it's all your fault
* Rachel Mendelson, who understands
* Theo and Clemmie, for the greenhouse and cobra beans
* Taki, Martha, Tina, Jean, Elaine, as always
* Pat, much missed, and Tim Bates, Gabrielle Dalton and especially Rosie McFadzean, my gardening friends, for their generosity and knowledge
* Claire Baldwin, for her help
* Jane C, Jane H and Sandra T, without whom
* Maria Rejt and Camilla Elworthy, whose support for my novels led to the *Financial Times* interview by Hannah Beckerman, in which my garden obsession was first laid bare
* Aitch, for the gorgeous cover
* Peter Straus, for his advice
* Kyle Cathie, whose idea this was, Judith Hannam and everyone at Kyle Books, for all their hard work
* And most of all Joanna Briscoe, for her tolerance, her encouragement and, increasingly, her extremely dangerous enabling, with my love

THE BLACKLIST

Each of these books, whether cookery, gardening or, most dangerously, both, has contributed to my downfall. They will lead you astray; approach with caution.

Myrtle Allen: *The Ballymaloe Cookbook* (Gill & Macmillan, 1977)

Paul Barney: *Edulis Nursery catalogue 2012–13*

Matthew Biggs, Jekka McVicar and Bob Flowerdew: *The Complete Book of Vegetables, Herbs and Fruit* (Kyle Cathie 2006)

Ursula Buchan: *Garden People* (Thames & Hudson 2007)

Karel Čapek: *The Gardener's Year* (Modern Library 2002)

Beth Chatto: *Beth Chatto's Garden Notebook* (Orion 2011)
The Beth Chatto Handbook (2015)

Sue Clifford and Angela King: *The Apple Source Book* (Hodder & Stoughton 2007)

Margaret Costa: *Four Seasons Cookery Book* (Sphere 1972)

Martin Crawford: *Creating a Forest Garden* (Green Books 2010)

Alan Davidson: *The Oxford Companion to Food* (OUP 2006)

Jennifer Davies: *The Victorian Kitchen Garden* (BBC Books 1987)
The Wartime Kitchen and Garden (BBC Books 1993)

Mark Diacono: *A Taste of the Unexpected* (Quadrille 2010)
A Year At Otter Farm (Bloomsbury Publishing 2014)
The New Kitchen Garden (Saltyard Books 2015)

Ken Fern: *Plants for a Future* (Permanent Publications 2012)

Alys Fowler: *The Thrifty Forager* (Kyle Books 2011)
Abundance (Kyle Books 2013)

Patience Gray: *Honey from a Weed* (Lyons Press 1997)

Dorothy Hartley: *Food in England* (MacDonald and Jane's 1975)

Diana Henry: *Salt Sugar Smoke* (Mitchell Beazley 2012)

Sandor Ellix Katz: *Wild Fermentation* (Chelsea Green 2003)

Derek Jarman and Howard Sooley: *Derek Jarman's Garden* (Thames & Hudson 2002)

Joy Larkcom: *Oriental Vegetables* (John Murray 1997)
  Grow Your Own Vegetables (Frances Lincoln 2002)
  The Organic Salad Garden (Frances Lincoln 2003)
  Creative Vegetable Gardening (Mitchell Beazley 2008)
  Just Vegetating (Frances Lincoln 2012)
Christopher Lloyd: *Gardener Cook* (Frances Lincoln 1997)
Rory McEwen and Caroline Cuthbert: *The Botanical Paintings* (Royal Botanic Garden Edinburgh 1988)
Richard Mabey: *Flora Britannica* (Chatto & Windus 1997)
Tovah Martin: *The Unexpected Houseplant* (Timber Press 2012)
Joan Morgan and Alison Richards: *The Book of Apples* (Ebury 1993)
Adele Nozedar: *The Hedgerow Handbook* (Square Peg 2012)
Richard Olney: *Simple French Food* (John Wiley & Sons 1992)
Mirabel Osler: *A Gentle Plea for Chaos* (Bloomsbury Publishing 2011)
Eleanor Perényi: *Green Thoughts* (Pimlico 1994)
Roger Phillips: *Wild Food* (Macmillan 2014)
Nigel Slater: *Tender* Volume 1 (Fourth Estate 2009), Volume 2 (Fourth Estate 2010)
Soil Association Journal: *Mother Earth* Winter 1947–October 1971
Christopher Stocks: *Forgotten Fruits* (Windmill 2009)
Barbara M Walker: *The Little House Cookbook* (Harper Collins 1979)
Patrick Whitefield: *How To Make a Forest Garden* (Permanent Publications 1996)

INDEX